A Student-Friendly Guide to Move from Civil Law to U.S. Common Law

A Student-Friendly Guide to Move from Civil Law to U.S. Common Law

Nancy Daspit and Kirsten Schaetzel

University of Michigan Press
Ann Arbor

Published in the United States of America by the
University of Michigan Press

ISBN 978-0-472-04001-8 (print)
ISBN 978-0-472-22232-2 (e-book)

First published October 2025

Authorized Representative: Easy Access System Europe, Mustamäe tee 50, 10621 Tallinn, Estonia, gpsr.requests@easproject.com

Contents

Acknowledgments

The authors would like to thank their colleagues and students at Emory University School of Law for their insights and support during the development of this text. Specifically, we would like to thank Gillian Harris, Associate Director of Academic Programs, for her sage advice and for trying some of the exercises in her "U.S. History in a Legal Context" course. Her feedback was very helpful. We would also like to thank two LLM students. Marcel Beck, Ph.D., contributed information and insights into the German legal system and gave us feedback on several sections of the text. Rabia Dogruyol contributed information and insights into the Turkish legal system. We thank them all for their assistance in making this text as clear and comprehensive as possible.

We would also like to thank Elizabeth Christian, Law Librarian for Research Services, for her research assistance in certain areas covered in this text, and Crystal Lee, Access Services Specialist, for assistance with copyright clearances, both in the Hugh F. McMillan Law Library. In addition, we want to thank Jeannette Livingston, Program Coordinator, who was an immense help in editing several portions of this text.

We also thank the entire team working with us at the University of Michigan Press for bringing this text to fruition. We are especially thankful for Katie La Plant for her guidance, patience, and support throughout the ups and downs of our publication journey. Her encouragement and willingness to share her time and expertise were more than commendable. We would also like to thank Juliette Snyder for her superb editorial support, explanations, and help. She always put a positive spin on any change.

Finally, we would like to thank our significant others, family, friends, and pets. The time we needed away from you to develop, write, and revise this text was significant at times. Thank you for your understanding and support.

There are many others, too numerous to mention by name, who helped us along this journey. Thank you for your ideas and guidance.

List of Figures

Preface

This book evolved from the authors' experiences teaching international students from civil code countries seeking a master's degree in law (LLM) in the United States. While these students come to the United States as lawyers—either as recent graduates in law or practicing attorneys—many are surprised at the differences between law practice and legal education in their home countries and practice and legal education in the United States. In addition to studying in a different language, these students are faced with new cultural norms, a different legal education protocol, and the concepts of dual sovereignty and precedent cases, among other legal norms taken for granted in the United States. All of these differences can be overwhelming and students often look for a concise guide to understanding them.

The authors gratefully acknowledge our colleagues who preceded us in providing guidance and explanations in several outstanding texts that traverse these differences. However, we discovered when we assigned some of those sources for coursework or supplemental readings to help the students transition into a common law legal mindset that they often did not have the time or energy to read much supplemental material. Comments such as, "we already have so much to read for our [doctrinal] classes," or "can't you just give us a shorter explanation or a diagram that illustrates all of this?" often left us scrambling to create such materials.

After much consideration, along with trial and error that provided us with abundant feedback from our students, the result is the information and materials in this text. It is not intended as a "be all/end all" for an international LLM student wanting to succeed in a U.S. law curriculum; rather, we have attempted to set out some key concepts, fundamental terminology, and practice examples to help the students transition into a U.S. common law environment; however, the text does include numerous citations to those outstanding texts mentioned above, so students can read for more detailed information as time permits.

This text can be used by non–U.S. lawyers as a stand-alone source to provide an introduction to legal education and law practice in the United States. It can also be used as the basis for introductory/transition courses covering legal research, analysis, and writing. The authors suggest, however, that professors/instructors teaching such courses should supplement with additional problem sets and instructional materials, such as power points and group exercises. Professors and instructors are the best sources to help students understand the differences in legal education and legal systems; this text is intended to introduce students to those differences and give students an organized and coherent "jumping-off point" in their understandings.

We wish all professors, instructors, students, and lawyers using this text success in understanding the characteristics and criteria inherent in the common law system of the United States. We hope this text will play a small part in their future legal study and endeavors.

Chapter 1
Overview of American Common Law

Introduction

You probably chose this book because you want to learn more about the U.S. common law system. If that is your reason for reading this book, you made a good choice. This book is, as its title says, a student-friendly guide to transition from civil law to common law practice. There are other books on the market that are more extensive and detailed; many of them are noted in the footnotes. However, the purpose of this book is to give an overview of the most significant characteristics of the U.S. common law system and to introduce the main features of legal education and legal writing in the United States.

To appreciate the differences between how the law operates in a civil code jurisdiction and in a common law jurisdiction, it is helpful to understand the environment in which the common law developed and has since evolved, as well as some fundamental differences between the two systems.[1]

The term "common law" has two meanings that are sometimes confused. First, "common law" can mean a source of law on which a court relies for a legal decision. This meaning applies when there is no statute[2] governing the legal issue, and the attorneys and court must rely solely on legal rules established

1. For more detailed historical background, refer to the Bibliography.

2. In the United States, the term "statute" is usually used instead of the term "code" when referring to legislation.

by courts in precedent cases (previous court decisions on the same issue) to analyze a legal issue and reach a decision. The other meaning of the term "common law" conveys a broader concept—it refers to the method for judicial decision making—the entire system of case law that pervades the legal system.[3]

Civil code jurisdictions evolved from the law of the citizens of Rome, to the French Civil Code (circa 1804), and the German Civil Code (circa 1896). The concepts and structure from the French code spread through most Latin countries in Europe and the Americas, as well as the French, Portuguese, Spanish, and Dutch colonies in Africa, the Middle East, and Asia. The German code spread through what are now Austria, Switzerland, Eastern Europe, Japan, Korea, and Taiwan.[4]

In contrast, the common law originated in England from the law of the "royal courts" first established after the Norman Conquest (circa 1066). The decisions from these courts eventually became laws that were "common to the entire kingdom." Over time, as these royal courts addressed similar legal issues, the laws (the "legal rules") became consistent, although the facts were unique in each case. These laws evolved over time through the cases heard by these royal courts. The British spread the common law, in one form or another, to their numerous colonies.[5]

There are four key differences between a civil law jurisdiction and a common law jurisdiction: (1) the legal authority used in a legal analysis, (2) the structure of the legal analysis, (3) the language and structure of legislation (codified law), and (4) the legal education methodologies.[6]

Regarding the first two differences, "legal analysis" refers to the logic/reasoning used to answer a legal question, and "legal authority" refers to the sources of law needed to answer a legal question. Both civil law and common law jurisdictions have constitutions, which are considered the highest legal authority in the jurisdiction. In a civil law system, legal authority additional to the constitution is the code, and the principle means for legal analysis relies on deductive reasoning.[7]

---

3. Case law governs all legal decisions, even those that rely on a statute, a regulation, or a constitutional provision as the source of the legal rule that determines the outcome of the issue.

4. Jane C. Ginsburg, *Legal Methods,* Part I § D.1, p. 72–73 (5th ed. 2020); Nadia E. Nedzel, *Legal Reasoning, Research, and Writing for International Graduate Students*, Ch. 1 § I.A, p. 27 (5th ed. 2021).

5. Ginsburg, *supra,* pp.70–72. Adaptions were often made to incorporate local law and customs, so some countries now have hybrid systems. *See also* Peter Hay, *Law of the United States,* Ch. 1 § I.A.1 (4th ed. 2016); Nedzel, *supra,* Ch. 1 § I.A.1, p. 27.

6. Ginsburg, *supra,* Part I § D.2, pp. 74–77.

7. Nedzel, *supra,* Ch. 1 § 1.A, p. 29.

In contrast, legal authority in a common law system includes both primary authority (the source of the law) and secondary authority, which discusses, describes, and analyzes the law (e.g., treatises and periodicals). Legal analysis in a common law system includes inductive, deductive, and comparative reasoning.[8] These concepts of legal authority and legal analysis are discussed more thoroughly in Chapters 2 and 5, respectively.

Briefly, legislation in civil code countries (codes) is drafted broadly, relying usually on general and abstract principles, which allows for application to cover both the letter and the spirit of the law. In contrast, legislation in common law countries (statutes) is drafted using specific terms, sometimes even including specific examples, to ensure clarity when applying a statute to facts in a particular case. Common law courts sometimes will conclude that a statute does not apply because the language in the statute does not clearly show any explicit or implied intent to cover the factual situation at issue.[9]

Relevant examples for broadly drafted statutes in civil code countries can be found, for instance, in German, Swiss, Turkish, and French tort laws. In Germany, section 823 paragraph 1 of the German Civil Code ("Bürgerliches Gesetzbuch")[10] applies to a broad variety of tort law cases rather than applying only to specific, discrete tort scenarios. It is up to the courts to define the particular elements and the kinds of conduct these statutes should cover. With Article 41 of the Swiss Civil Code ("Obligationenrecht"), Switzerland has enacted a similar statute.[11] Compared to the German statute, the Swiss statute is even more broadly drafted because it does not state the wrongdoer's liability only with respect to specific protected individual rights.

Similarly, the broadly drafted Article 49 of the Turkish Code of Obligations ("Türk Borçlar Kanunu") defines tort liability as fault, an unlawful act, causal link, and damage. However, the law does not explicitly define these elements. While the code states that anyone causing loss or damage unlawfully must compensate the injured party, it does not clarify what constitutes unlawfulness. As such, it is up to the courts to interpret the law and apply the interpretation to particular facts.

---

8. Nedzel, *supra*, Ch. 3, § I, p. 86. Comparative reasoning is also sometimes called "analogical reasoning," although it includes comparisons showing differences (distinctions) as well as analogies (similarities).

9. *See* Ginsburg, *supra,* pp. 75–77.

10. Section 823 paragraph 1 German Civil Code states: "Any person who intentionally or negligently causes unlawful injury to the life, limb, health, liberty, property or other right of another shall be liable to compensate the other for any resulting damage."

11. Art. 41 Swiss Civil Code states: "Whoever unlawfully causes damage to another, whether intentionally or through negligence, shall be liable to compensate him."

One of the most broadly drafted tort laws in civil code countries can be found in French tort law, Article 1382 French Civil Code ("Code Civil"),[12] which focuses mainly on damages resulting from the wrongdoer's conduct. It omits from its wording any intentional requirement for the alleged wrongdoer's actions, as well as the unlawfulness of the conduct.

Additionally, because of the above three differences (the legal authority used in a legal analysis, the structure of the legal analysis, and the language and structure of legislation), the legal education systems also differ. Generally, in civil law systems, classes are predominantly lecture based (magisterial), and students are not expected to read ahead to prepare for class. In addition, law school exams rely almost entirely on memorization and regurgitation of the memorized material; very little actual analysis of legal questions is required.[13] Further, in many countries, the education systems, and in particular law school education systems, rely very little on electronic materials and computerized systems for registration and communication between and among professors and students. These differing education methodologies and the amount of reliance on technology in education may introduce additional novel systems and procedures in which international students studying in the United States need to gain proficiency.

In contrast, in the U.S. common law jurisdiction, the law is learned through dialog—the Socratic Method of instruction, which differs from the magisterial instruction in civil code countries. In Socratic Method classes, students read legal cases before class and their professor asks them questions about the cases during class. Through this dialog, students learn the rule of law to be applied to the facts and can see the legal analysis that was used in applying this rule to these facts. The professor can point out analogies (similarities) and distinctions (differences) between the cases' facts and legal reasoning applied. This Socratic Method of teaching reinforces the importance of case law—and facts—in common law legal analysis. Further, the Socratic Method requires the students to practice their legal reasoning skills. During the course of the dialog, the professor will often change the facts from those in the case under discussion, creating a hypothetical, or "hypo," and ask the students what the result would be with the new facts and possibly even whether the law itself is still "good law"—does it still serve its purpose? In addition, law school exams in the U.S. common law require the students to analyze hypothetical factual situations and apply the legal rules, as appropriate, to

---

12. Art. 1382 French Civil Code states: "Any conduct of a person that causes damage to another obligates the wrongdoer to pay damages if at fault."

13. *See Ginsburg, supra* at 77; Nedzel, *supra,* Ch. 1 § I.A, pp. 29–30; Hay, *supra,* Appx. 3 § I.

those facts and predict a likely outcome.[14] (More about U.S. legal education in Chapter 3.)

In addition, a law degree is a bachelor's degree everywhere in the world except in the United States, Canada, and a few other scattered institutions, where it is a post-bachelor's degree.[15] Note, however, that England, although it is a common law country, usually follows the rest of the world in awarding the first law degree as a bachelor's degree.

Key Concepts 1: The following concepts are significant in understanding the U.S. common law system. Read over the definitions given below and then choose the appropriate concept for each blank in the exercise that follows. Check your answers with the Answer Key in Appendix A.

1. *common law*: a body of law that is based on custom and principles and embodied in case law and that serves as precedent or is applied to situations not covered by statute
2. *civil code*: contains the basic law of persons, property, obligations, donations, and successions that statutes must accord with and judges must apply in deciding cases
3. *inductive reasoning (induction)*: inference of a generalized conclusion from particular instances
4. *deductive reasoning (deduction)*: inference in which the conclusion about particulars follows necessarily from general or universal premises
5. *Socratic Method*: (noun) a technique of philosophical discussion—and of law-school instruction—by which the questioner (a law professor) questions one or more followers (the law students), building on each answer with another question, especially an analogy incorporating the answer. This method takes its name from the Greek philosopher Socrates, who lived in Athens from about 469–399 BC. His method is a traditional one in law schools, primarily because it forces law students to think through issues rationally and deductively—a skill required in the practice of law
6. *lecture-based*: (adjective) a discourse delivered to an audience or class especially for instruction
7. *hypothetical/"hypo"*: involving or being based on a suggested idea (in law classes, a "hypo" is a similar case to the one being studied with one or two facts changed)

---

14. Nedzel, *supra,* Ch. 1 § 1.A, pp. 29–30. In most essay exam questions, there is no single "yes there is a claim" or "no there is no claim" answer. The student earns points toward the final grade by demonstrating their analytical ability to support their answer.

15. In the United States, a law degree is a "Juris Doctor" (JD). Hay, *supra,* Appx. 3 § I.

8. *precedent*: (noun) a legal decision that should be followed by a judge when deciding a later similar case
9. *analogy*: (noun) a comparison of two otherwise unlike things based on a similarity of a particular aspect or trait; *to analogize*: (verb) to make such a comparison
10. *distinction*: (noun) a comparison of two things that are legally different from each other in a particular aspect or trait; *to distinguish*: (verb) to make such a comparison

Use one of the concepts above in each of the following sentences:

1. Classes at American law schools are characterized by the ____________ ____________, and students sometimes get nervous about professors asking them questions over the cases they read.
2. Sometimes when examining the logic of a court's decisions in two cases, it's most helpful to look at the ________________ between two cases.
3. In many law schools, including some in the United States, professors conduct ______________________ classes, telling the students what they need to know about cases.
4. When trying to figure out how a client's claim will be decided in court, lawyers must look at ______________________ cases to see how judges have decided similar claims in the past. Lawyers then _______ ________________ their current case with precedent cases to see the similarities in the cases.
5. Making an ________________ between two cases makes for sound, strong legal reasoning because similarities between your case and a precedent case show how your case will probably be decided.
6. The legal system in the United States is a ____________________ system as principles in case law are applied as precedent to current cases.
7. After going over the cases in the assigned reading, the professor introduced several ______________________ and asked students if these might be decided in the same way as the assigned cases.
8. Using ______________ reasoning, we can examine a judge's past sentencings and get an idea of how long a defendant may be sentenced if found guilty.
9. Most countries have __________________ legal systems, which rely more on applying statutes rather than precedent.
10. Sometimes lawyers use ________________ reasoning when hearing a potential client's story; they put together the details of the story to figure out what happened in order to decide whether or not to take the case.

A. U.S. Common Law Environment

In addition to the historical background, to understand legal analysis and research in the United States—and to understand how the application of precedent cases affects this analysis and research—you need to be familiar with how the judiciary operates in the U.S. common law system. Thus, you should understand the basic organizational principles of the federal and state government systems in the United States and how the judiciary fits within each of these systems, as well as the separate, but parallel, operation of the federal and state court systems in the United States.

1. The Tripartite System of Government and Federalism[16]

The United States is a federation of states with powers shared between the federal government and the governments of each state.[17] The U.S. Constitution delineates the powers of the federal government, and any powers not prescribed in the Constitution are reserved for the states.[18] The term "federalism" applies to this relationship—often tense—between the federal government and the governments of the states.[19] Each state, as well as the federal government, is thus considered an "independent sovereign" capable of defining and enforcing its own laws, subject to the limits of the U.S. Constitution and the Full Faith and Credit Clause of the U.S. Constitution.[20] Hence, the term "dual sovereignty" is also used to describe this structure. This concept of dual

---

16. *See generally,* Margaret Z. Johns & Rex R. Perschbacher, *The United States Legal System*, Ch. 3 (3rd ed. 2012).

17. For simplicity's sake, this text will address only 49 states and the District of Columbia; it will not address the U.S. territories—Puerto Rico, Guam, the U.S. Virgin Islands, American Samoa, and the North Mariana Islands. This text also will not address the U.S. state of Louisiana because it is primarily a civil law jurisdiction, although some areas of its laws have been influenced by common law, particularly its criminal code and, to varying extents, its administrative law and civil procedure. https://libguides.law.lsu.edu/c.php?g=693022#.-txt=Louisiana (last visited February 2, 2024).

18. U.S. Const. Bill of Rights, amend. 10.

19. *See generally*, 16A Am. Jur 2d *Constitutional Law* § 214 *Federalism and the Powers Reserved to the States* (West 2023). Questions abound regarding what powers are "reserved to the states" within various areas of the law, and thus this has been the subject of much scholarly debate. *See, e.g.*, Thomas L. Chittum, III, *Can You Hear Me Now? Cell Phone Jamming and The Tenth Amendment*, Note, 13 Nev. L.J. 257 (Fall 2012); Kurt T. Lash, *James Madison's Celebrated Report of 1800: The Transformation of the Tenth Amendment*, 74 Geo. Wash. L. Rev. 165 (Feb. 2006).

20. U.S. Const., art. IV, cl. 1 ("Full Faith and Credit shall be given in each State to the public Acts, Records, and judicial Proceedings of every other State. And the Congress may by general Laws prescribe the Manner in which such Acts, Records and Proceedings shall be proved, and the Effect thereof.")

sovereignty is significant to understanding the operation of the federal and state court systems in the United States.[21]

The federal government, as well as each state government, is organized into a three-part structure: the executive branch, the legislative branch, and the judicial branch. As indicated below, there is a system of "checks and balances" among the three branches, designed to ensure that no one branch has—or can seize—full control of the operation of the government.[22]

a. The Executive Branch of Government

The executive branch is charged with executing the laws of the "sovereign"—the federal government or an individual state government. At the federal level, this branch includes the president of the United States, the vice president, the secretaries in the president's cabinet, and the administrative agencies. At the state level, this branch includes the governor of the state, the lieutenant governor, and the administrative agencies.[23] Among the key powers for the "chief executive"—the president or the governor—are the powers to propose legislation and budgets, to veto legislation, and to ensure that the enacted laws are carried out.

The administrative agencies are generally the means through which many of the laws are executed.[24] Virtually all agencies enact "laws"—called "regulations" or "rules" to distinguish them from statutes—that facilitate the orderly implementation of the functions for which the agency was created.[25] For example, the Internal Revenue Service (IRS) is the agency responsible for collecting social security (federal retirement) and federal income taxes from the public. In order to do this, the IRS has developed procedures and a series of forms, with their instructions, to facilitate an orderly and timely collection of taxes. These regulations generally carry the same force of law as statutes and are subject to interpretation and constitutional scrutiny by the courts. In addition to their regulatory functions, some federal and state agencies

---

21. *See* sections B & C, *infra,* in this chapter.

22. For a more detailed description of each branch of government, see Hay, *supra,* Ch. 2 § A.II; Johns, *supra,* Ch. 3.

23. Although some states refer to some of the agency heads as "secretary" (e.g., secretary of state), many of these agency heads have other titles, such as director or commissioner.

24. *See, generally,* Ginsburg, *supra,* Part 1 § C, pp. 63–69. Each federal and state agency operates under the authority of laws enacted by the legislative branch of government, specifically, the Administrative Procedures Act, 5 U.S.C.A. §§ 500–596 (West 2023).

25. The specific procedures for the creation of administrative regulations and the operations of agencies are set out at 5 U.S.C.A. §§ 551–559; *see also* Ginsburg, *supra,* Part 1 § C.2 (adjudication) and § C.3 (rule promulgation).

also have powers to adjudicate disputes arising under their regulations.[26] For example, disputes arising about the eligibility for and the amount of social security (federal retirement) payments are first submitted to an adjudicative body (or person) within the agency; if the claimant is dissatisfied with that decision, then they may take the matter to a court within the judicial branch of government.[27]

The powers of the executive branch are subject to limitations—part of the "checks and balances" included in the U.S. Constitution and carried into the constitutions for every state. For example, when the chief executive, president, or governor vetoes legislation (a "check" on the power of the legislative branch), the legislative branch can override that veto (the countervailing "balance") if the legislators garner the appropriate number of votes to override the veto.[28]

b. The Legislative Branch of Government

The legislative branch of government is responsible to propose, debate, and enact laws. At the federal level, the legislative branch is the U.S. Congress, which is a bicameral (two-part) body that includes the Senate and the House of Representatives. Each state elects two senators, and it elects its U.S. representatives based on the population within the state. Thus, the number of representatives from each state is reevaluated every ten years, after the U.S. Census is taken.

Forty-nine of the states have a legislative branch similarly organized into a bicameral body; only Nebraska is unicameral.[29] Generally, in the states this branch is called the "Legislature" or the "General Assembly." The titles "senator" and "representative" are often used in the states, and the electoral scheme in a state is similar to the federal scheme for each "senatorial" district and geographic "representative" district.[30]

As with the powers of the executive branch, the powers of the legislative branch are also subject to limitations. The "checks" include the executive branch's veto power over laws enacted by the legislative branch[31] and the

---

26. Ginsburg, *supra*, Part 1 § C.2.

27. *Id.*

28. Johns, *supra*, Ch. 2, § 3.2.2, p. 91.

29. For more information about Nebraska's unicameral legislature, see https://nebraskalegislature.gov/about/about.php.

30. E. Allen Farnsworth, *An Introduction to the Legal System of the United States*, pp. 75–76 (4th ed. 2010).

31. Johns, *supra*, fn. 26.

judicial branch's scrutiny of a law to ensure that a law is constitutional.[32] For the "balances," the legislative body can override an executive veto with sufficient votes. Also, if the legislative body does not agree with an interpretation of a statute by a court within its jurisdiction, that legislative body can enact or amend the statute effective **prospectively**,[33] which essentially overrules[34] the court's decision as it applies going forward; however, the legislative body cannot enact or amend a statute overruling only the specific court decision that it disagrees with. Similarly, if a court has determined a statute is unconstitutional, the legislative body can only amend the statute (or repeal it and pass a new statute) that eliminates the constitutional defect; it cannot merely overrule the court.[35]

c. The Judicial Branch of Government

The judicial branch of government consists of the various courts authorized by constitution or by statute to adjudicate cases as described here. A court's chief responsibility is to interpret and apply the laws—both statutory and common law legal rules. Through this interpretation, a court will decide the disputes arising between or among the parties in the case, and it can determine the constitutionality of a law.

Accordingly, a court's three main functions are as follows:

a. Interpret the law—statutory, regulatory, and common law,
b. Decide the dispute between or among the parties, and
c. Determine the constitutionality of a law, when at issue.

Because courts can interpret the laws, this provides flexibility for the law to evolve, permitting a court to address novel facts not previously considered, advances in technology that affect the circumstances giving rise to a dispute, or changing societal norms. This type of court-based evolution is a significant characteristic of the common law. It allows the law—whether a law is statutory, regulatory, or common law—to adapt much more quickly than it could if the only recourse for changing the law was a legislative process.

---

32. Johns, *supra*, Ch. 3 § 3.2.2(c)(iii), p. 102.

33. Toni M. Fine, *American Legal System: A Resources and Reference Guide*, Ch. 1 § I.1.d – § I.2, p. 25 (1997).

34. In this context, "overrules" means the legislative body has rejected and replaced the legal rule used in a court decision. This does not change the outcome in that particular case; however, for all future cases raising the legal issue, the new rule would be applied to resolve the issue.

35. Fine, *supra*, Ch. I § I.1.d, p. 25.

At the federal level, the President appoints judges, but the nominations are subject to approval (ratification) by the Senate. At the state level, the selection processes for judges vary.[36] Some states use a system modeled from the federal system, with a governor appointing judges subject to ratification by all or part of the legislative body. Other states elect judges. And some states use a combination of the two systems, with a governor appointing a judge for a newly created judgeship or to replace a retiring judge prior to an election, with the appointed judge then subject to a ratification election. Note that when this ratification election occurs, many states allow other candidates to run against the appointed judge.

2. The System of Checks and Balances—Judicial Branch Scrutiny

Although the idea of "checks and balances" among the three government branches was briefly described above, of particular note for this book are the actions allowed by the judicial branch of government to review the actions of the executive and legislative branches of government.[37] The chart below describes the actions allowed by the court.

Actions of the Legislative or Executive Branch	**Judicial Branch Scrutiny**
Legislative body passes law	Is the law constitutional?
Legislative body creates an agency & authorizes it to act	Is the delegation to the agency constitutional? (i.e., did the legislative body delegate too much of its law-making authority to an agency?)
Administrative agency issues rules & regulations	Are the rules and regulations constitutional?
The agency resolves disputes via its adjudicative process	Is this action consistent with a legislature's delegation of authority? Is this action consistent with case law in this area of law?

(continued)

36. For more detailed information regarding the selection of state judges, refer to J.R. Swanegan & Ellen S. Podgor, *Overview of U.S.*, Ch. 1 § II.C.2.d, p. 14, *Law,* Ch. 1 §§ B-C (2nd ed. 2019); *see also* https://ballotpedia.org/Judicial_selection_in_the_states (last visited February 2, 2024).

37. Johns, *supra*, Ch. 3 § 3.2.2(c)(iii), p.102 (the early case of *Marbury v. Madison*, 5 U.S. (1 Cranch) 137 (1802) is credited as the source for this "doctrine of judicial review"); *see also* Fine, *supra*, Ch. I § I.1.2, p. 25; Nedzel, *supra*, Ch. 2 § III.4.a., pp. 59–60.

(continued)

Actions of the Legislative or Executive Branch	**Judicial Branch Scrutiny**
If a legislative body or administrative agency takes one of the following actions: • codifies case law, • modifies case law by enacting or amending a statute or regulation, or • overrules case law by enacting a statute or regulation (except when the case determined the law had a constitutional defect, which would require a rewrite of the law to eliminate the defect).	Then such actions would be similarly subject to judicial review, as described above.

B. Structure and Operation of the Federal and State Court Systems

Introduction

The federal court system and most of the state court systems are organized in the tri-level structure described in the chart below:

Federal	**Type of Court**	**States**[38]
U.S. Supreme Court	**Court of last resort**	Generally called the Supreme Court in that state
U.S. Courts of Appeals (circuit courts)	**Intermediate appellate courts**	Often called Courts of Appeals
U.S. District Courts	**Trial level courts**	Often called State Courts, Superior Courts, County Courts
e.g., Bankruptcy Court, Tax Court	**Specialty courts**[39]	e.g., Probate Court, Juvenile Court

38. Many state court systems are tri-level; however, the following states have a bi-level court system: Delaware, the District of Columbia, Montana, Nevada, New Hampshire, North Dakota, Rhode Island, South Dakota, Vermont, and Wyoming. In addition, the names for courts in the states will vary. For example, New York uses the title "Court of Appeals" for this highest court. Strangely enough, the trial level court in New York is called the Supreme Court, and the intermediate appellate court is the Appellate Division of the Supreme Court. Similarly, the names for the trial level courts differ from state to state.

39. Specialty courts may or may not be considered at precisely the same level as a trial court. For example, some trial courts may hear appeals from specialty courts and/or must approve decisions from some specialty courts. In addition, a decision from a federal bankruptcy court is usually first appealed to the U.S. district court in the same district as the bankruptcy court.

There are five fundamental differences between the operation of the court systems in the United States and the courts' operation in civil law systems in other countries.[40] First, the American legal system is an "adversarial system"; each side in a court case opposes the other side—they are adversaries to each other, The court[41] addresses only actual disputes (controversies) between parties; it can never issue an "advisory" opinion or address any matter that raises only a political question.[42]

Second, in the entry level courts (trial and specialty courts) the court's role is passive in a given case.[43] At trial, the attorneys bear the responsibility to identify and frame the legal issues, to find and introduce evidence, and to advocate for their respective clients.[44] This is different from civil law court systems, which are often termed "inquisitorial," meaning the judge can play an active role in questioning witnesses and determining the truth from the evidence offered during the proceedings.[45]

Third, American trial and specialty courts can rely on a "jury,"[46] a group of 6 or 12 ordinary citizens (called "jurors") who listen to all the evidence, deliberate in private, and then render a "verdict"[47] in a particular case.[48] Once the attorneys have presented all the evidence, and prior to the jurors leaving the courtroom to deliberate in private, the court instructs the jury on the law applicable

40. The comparisons here are based on civil law systems generally. Because each civil law jurisdiction has its own structure and operational rules, comparisons to specific civil law jurisdictions would be too numerous to cover. *See* Nedzel, *supra*, ch.1 § IB, for comparisons to Islamic law, Asian legal traditions, and Marxist/Leninist theories.

41. In the United States, lawyers use the term "the court" when referring to cases; reference is never made to "the judge" or "the judges." This avoids any perception that the arguments made by the lawyers are personal or that a decision by a court is personal.

42. Toni Jaeger-Fine, *The U.S. Legal System: The Basics*, Ch. 3 § C.1.d, pp. 39–41 (2021).

43. Fine, *supra,* Ch. 1 § D.2, p. 7.

44. Swanegan, *supra,* Ch. 1 § II.B, p. 8.

45. *Id.* at p. 9.

46. *See,* Nedzel, *supra,* Ch. 1 § II, B.3; *see also* M. Baffy & K. Schaetzel, *Academic Legal Discourse and Analysis*, Part II, Ch. 1.C, pp. 194–97.

47. The "verdict" is the decision by the jury. From the verdict, the court issues a "judgment," which documents the terms that are enforceable by law. Most state trial level courts do not publish case opinions, even if the court decided the case instead of a jury. However, the federal trial level courts, a rare few state trial level courts, and some federal and state specialty courts, do issue case opinions. Opinions from trial level courts are not precedents, however.

48. At the trial level, the parties in a case (or the defendant in a criminal case) can request that the judge, instead of a jury, hears the case and decides the matter. This is known as a "bench trial"—where the judge would "find the facts" and render a decision by applying the law to those facts. At the appellate level in both the federal and state court systems, however, there are no juries. Additionally, in the United States, in both federal and state

to the case.[49] During its private deliberations, the jury determines the credibility of the witnesses and decides the "truth" from the evidence in the case. After this "finding of facts," the jury then applies the law—in accordance with the court's instructions—to those facts and reaches its verdict. During the course of a trial, the court solves only those legal questions explicitly put before it—for example, whether to admit or exclude particular evidence.

Fourth, in a civil law jurisdiction, there can be "lay" judges—judges who are not lawyers. In contrast, in a common law jurisdiction, there are no "lay"[50] judges at any level of federal and state courts.[51] However, judges in any of the trial courts—federal or state—sometimes will appoint a "special master," a person who is considered an expert in a particular field, when the court believes such expertise would help the court better understand the complexities of a case. A "special master" is not required to be an attorney; for example, the court might appoint a certified public accountant (CPA) in a dispute involving the valuation of a business or a case involving tax fraud.

Fifth, perhaps the greatest difference between the U.S. common law and civil law court systems is the concept of "federalism" (sometimes called "dual sovereignty") in which the federal and state government systems, including the court systems, operate independently of each other. Furthermore, although there are statutes in both the federal and state jurisdictions in the United States, when any part of a statute requires interpretation, it is a court in that jurisdiction that will determine the applicable interpretation.[52] Thus, lawyers and judges rely on court opinions, and in particular precedent

---

jurisdictions, fewer and fewer of the cases filed in courts are decided by a trial—either a jury trial or a bench trial. For example, less than 2% of the federal criminal cases went to trial during the twelve-month period ending March 2020. The percentage of civil cases resolved by a jury dropped from 5.5% in 1962 to 0.8% in 2013. The rest of the civil cases are decided through motion practice, settlement by the parties, mediation, or arbitration; in criminal cases, defendants often reach plea agreements and thus avoid a trial. Emanuella Evans, *Jury Trials are Disappearing. Here's Why,* Injustice Watch, Feb. 17, 2021, at https://www.injusticewatch.org/news/2021/disappearing-jury-trials-study/ (last visited February 2, 2024).

49. The court provides the definitions and descriptions of the law that the jury must apply to the facts in the case at issue.

50. Under current law, only a licensed attorney can become a judge. Swanegan, *supra,* Ch. 1 § C.2.d, p. 14.

51. *Id.*

52. A court's interpretation of a statute is governed by a hierarchy of guidelines: First, courts look to the plain language of a statute. If this analysis leaves any uncertainty, the courts then turn to the Canons of Statutory Construction. Additionally, a court might review the legislative history of the statute. Eva H. Hanks, *Elements of Law,* Ch. 9 (2nd ed. 2010); *see also* Johns, *supra,* Ch. 3; Nedzel, *supra,* Ch. 7 § V.

opinions, to maintain predictability and continuity in the law. The concepts of federalism and precedent are discussed more thoroughly in the following sections, B.2 and C.1–2, respectively.

1. Case Progression Example for a Federal Civil Case[53]

Figure 1.1 describes what happens—from beginning to end—in a civil matter within the federal jurisdiction. This description can generally apply to the events in a state jurisdiction as well, with only the court names being different.[54]

Prior to the initiation of a lawsuit, something happens[55] (referred to as "the Big Bang" on Figure 1.1). "The Big Bang" just means something happened (e.g., a tort or a contract dispute) to cause one or both parties to seek the services of an attorney), which brings the client to the lawyer or law firm. The client tells the lawyer what happened and asks for advice. It is at this point that the process of legal and factual research will begin for the lawyer. The lawyer will look at the story presented by the client, likely seek additional witnesses to interview, and try to draft a complete picture of the events. As the lawyer is doing this, she is also looking at what possible legal claims the client might have, as well as the possible defenses to these claims. At this point, the lawyer (or her associate) will draft a legal memorandum, which is an objective analysis of the facts, the claims and defenses, and the likely outcome if the matter were to proceed into court. This objective analysis will be the main subject of Chapter 3.

Assuming the firm accepts the case, it will file a complaint, and the client now is the plaintiff in the case. This complaint is filed in a federal district court—a trial level court—to initiate a case.[56] The defendant can then file a motion to dismiss[57] or an answer to the complaint. Once a defendant files the

53. Joan Coughlin, et al., *An Advocate Persuades,* Ch. 3 (2016); *see also* Deborah B. McGregor & Cynthia Adams, *The International Lawyer's Guide to Legal Analysis & Communication in the U.S.,* Ch. 3 § D (2008); Jaeger-Fine, *supra,* Ch. 6 §§ C-D.

54. Each state has its own court structure, so there may be some slight variations. For information about a specific state, go to that state's website and review the information about its court system. E.g., gerogiacourts.gov or iowacourts.gov.

55. For example, a contract dispute, a car accident, or a property dispute.

56. A case also could be initiated in one of the specialty courts by filing a complaint, but for purposes of this example, the case will start in a U.S. District Court.

57. Swanegan, *supra,* Ch. 5 § III.B.4.a, p. 154. Instead of filing an answer, a defendant could file a motion to dismiss some or all of the claims in the complaint. There are several bases on which the motion could be based—for example, lack of jurisdiction, improper venue, or "failure to state a claim on which relief can be granted." This latter example means that even if every allegation in the complaint were true, there is no legal basis that entitles the plaintiff to relief.

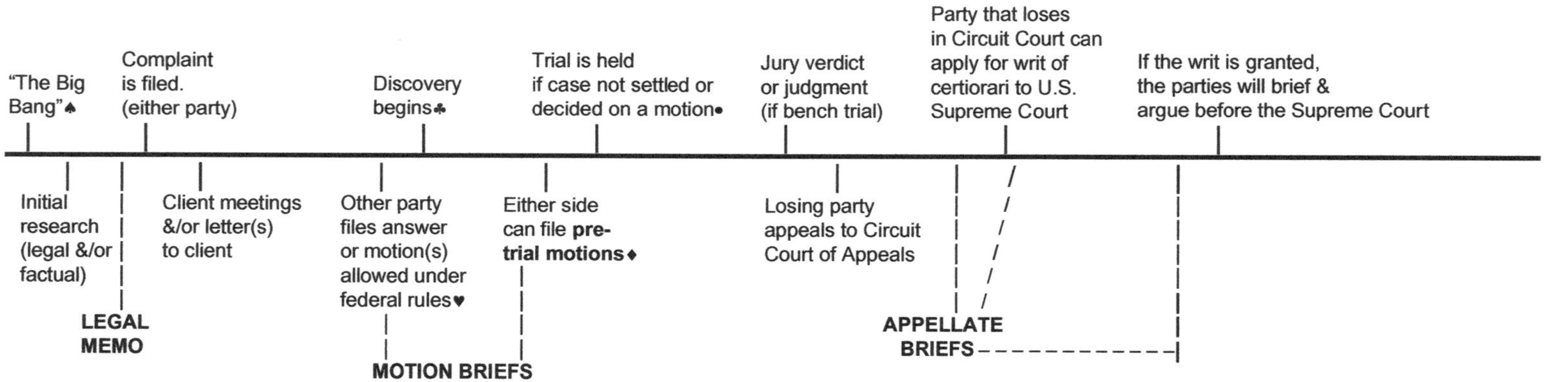

♠ **"The Big Bang" just means something happened (e.g., a tort or a contract dispute) to cause one or both parties to seek the services of an attorney.**

♣ **Once the complaint and answer are filed, both sides of the dispute are allowed to "discover" evidence from the other party. The means to do this include written interrogatories (questions), which require written answers; written requests for documents; written requests for admissions about the events [facts]; and depositions of the opposing party(ies) or potential witnesses. A "deposition" is a formal questioning by the attorney for one party of an opposing party or potential witness, where the person questioned is under oath and the entire proceeding is recorded by a court reporter.**

♥ **For example, the defendant could file a motion to dismiss the case before filing an answer.**

♦ **The most common pre-trial motions are motions for summary judgment (MSJ) and motions to suppress or allow evidence at trial. An MSJ asks the court to decide one or more of the claims in the case by reviewing evidence gathered during discovery. For an MSJ, the attorneys may request an opportunity to present oral arguments to the court, but granting such a request is virtually always discretionary with the court.**

• **Most cases in the U.S. never go to trial. They are decided by other means, such as by mediation or arbitration, by agreement between the parties (a settlement), or by an MSJ.**

Figure 1.1 Progress of a Federal Civil Case

answer, the discovery period begins. "Discovery" is the process through which opposing counsel can elicit information from the other side, using document requests, interrogatories, and depositions. The information provided in response to these means is provided under oath and thus has the same effect as testimony given at a trial.

Many/most cases are settled or decided without ever going to trial. The parties could agree—or the court could order the parties—to resolve the dispute through some means of alternative dispute resolution (ADR), such as mediation or arbitration.[58] Mediation involves the two sides trying to resolve their issues through cooperation and problem solving with a neutral third party serving as a mediator, a person who works to get the parties themselves to reach agreement.[59] In contrast, arbitration is a process similar to litigation, but the parties present their respective arguments to a neutral factfinder. Prior to the start of an arbitration, the two sides agree on whom this neutral person will be and on whether the fact-finder's decision would be binding on the parties or merely advisory.[60] Or either party in the case could file a motion for summary judgment once the discovery period ends.[61]

If the legal issues are not settled or decided by motion during this discovery and pretrial period, the case then proceeds to trial. At this trial level, a single judge presides over all matters relating to the case. If any disputes arise concerning discovery, or if any motions are made prior to trial, this single judge would decide the matter based on the written "briefs"[62] filed by the attorneys for each side, and possibly after hearing oral arguments by the attorneys. If the case does go to trial, either a jury would hear the matter[63] or the parties could decide to have a bench trial.[64]

---

58. McGregor, *supra,* Ch. 3 § C.

59. *Id.*

60. *Id.*

61. Swanegan, *supra,* Ch. 5 § III.B.6, p. 157. A motion for summary judgment (MSJ), unlike a motion to dismiss, can be filed by either party, or both parties (a cross-motion for summary judgment). The moving party argues that there are no "genuine issues of material fact" and that they are thus entitled to judgment in their favor. For a MSJ, the arguments are supported by evidence that was obtained during the discovery period.

62. A "brief" (or a "court brief") is an attorney's arguments to persuade the court why their respective side should win the motion.

63. In a civil matter, the verdict would be either "the defendant is liable" to the plaintiff for the harm alleged or "the defendant is not liable." The terms "guilty" and "not guilty" apply only in a criminal case.

64. Fine, *supra,* Ch. I § D.2. A "bench trial" means the judge acted as the trier of fact instead of having a jury.

While the state court system is completely separate from the federal court system, "districts"[65] in the federal system are physically located within states, with each state having at least one district. Many states, however, have more than a single district because of the volume of federal cases, the population of the state, or both. For example, the state of Georgia (which has a relatively large population) has three federal districts, but the state of Wyoming (which has a relatively small population) is only a single district. Each federal district includes several judges, which allows multiple cases to progress simultaneously through the court system for the jurisdiction and allows cases to be assigned to judges on a random basis.

When either party is dissatisfied with a verdict or decision from the trial level court, that party can appeal. There are many bases on which the dissatisfied party can appeal, including whether the court made an error of law during the proceedings or whether the law at issue is unconstitutional. The party who initiates the appeal is called the "appellant," while the party who opposes the appeal (who won at trial) is called the "appellee."

Most cases can be appealed from the district court "as a matter of right," meaning that the appellant needs only to file a notice of appeal with the appropriate U.S. Circuit Court of Appeals, the intermediate appellate court for that geographic part of the federal jurisdiction.[66] There are a few situations when an appellant must file a petition to the appellate court requesting permission for that court to hear an appeal, but those are rare at this first level of appeal.

At this intermediate appellate level, a three-judge panel usually hears each case, although occasionally all of the judges on the court will hear a case. When the court hears an appeal with a three-judge panel, the party who loses this intermediate appeal can file a motion for a hearing *en banc*—asking the full court to hear the appeal—prior to initiating the process to appeal to the highest court.

In the federal jurisdiction, the highest court is the U.S. Supreme Court. At this level, the decision to hear a case is virtually always discretionary, meaning the justices on the Supreme Court decide whether to hear the appeal or not. The party who lost the appeal must submit a petition for certiorari, and the successful party must submit a petition in opposition to certiorari. The Supreme Court then responds with a grant or a denial of certiorari. Most

65. The full title for a district court is, e.g., The U.S. District Court for the Northern District of Georgia.

66. The United States is divided into 13 circuits. See "Territorial Jurisdiction," *infra*, section B.3.c.

often, such petitions are denied.[67] As a general rule, the Supreme Court grants certiorari only in cases when there is a split among the decisions of the Circuit Courts of Appeals on a particular legal issue, when the issue could have national significance, or when the case could have precedential value.[68] When certiorari has been granted, cases are virtually always heard by all nine justices of the Supreme Court.[69] The Supreme Court generally takes several months after it hears the oral arguments before it issues its opinion in the case. If the Supreme Court denies certiorari, then the decision of the circuit court of appeals is the final decision in the case.

2. Federalism in the Court Systems

While each court system operates in the hierarchical structure described above, the federal and state court systems operate independently of each other. This independent operation is what we refer to as "federalism" (or "dual sovereignty"). A case initiated in a federal court virtually always stays within the federal jurisdiction. Similarly, a case initiated in a state court virtually always stays within the state jurisdiction, with an exception for "removal jurisdiction," which is described in the section describing "territorial jurisdiction" below.

Key Concepts 2: The following concepts are significant in understanding the U.S. common law system. Read over the definitions given below and then choose the appropriate concept for each blank in the exercise that follows. Check your answers with the Answer Key.

1. *dual sovereignty*: (adjective + noun) having more than one sovereign (as a state government and the federal government)
2. *adversarial system*: (adjective + noun) constituting or relating to a system of justice in which the two opposing parties in a case conduct the inquiries developing the facts of the litigant's case

---

67. For example, in 2017, the Court received 5,910 petitions for certiorari, and it granted only 165 of those petitions. https://supremecourtpress.com/chance_of_success.html.

68. *See* https://www.uscourts.gov/about-federal-courts/educational-resources/about-educational-outreach/activity-resources/supreme-1#:~:text=Writs%20of%20Certiorari&text=The%20Court%20usually%20is%20not,or%20could%20have%20precedential%20value (last visited February 2, 2024).

69. There are exceptions to the "full-justice requirement," however, usually involving procedural matters, questions preliminary to the appeal, or emergency petitions, although in very rare situations, a justice might recuse herself/himself. For example, early in her tenure, Justice Elena Kagan recused herself from about 20 cases because prior to her confirmation as a Justice on the Supreme Court, Justice Kagan had been the U.S. Solicitor General, and thus she had argued some of these same cases in prior hearings. *See also,* fn. 87, *infra*, this chapter.

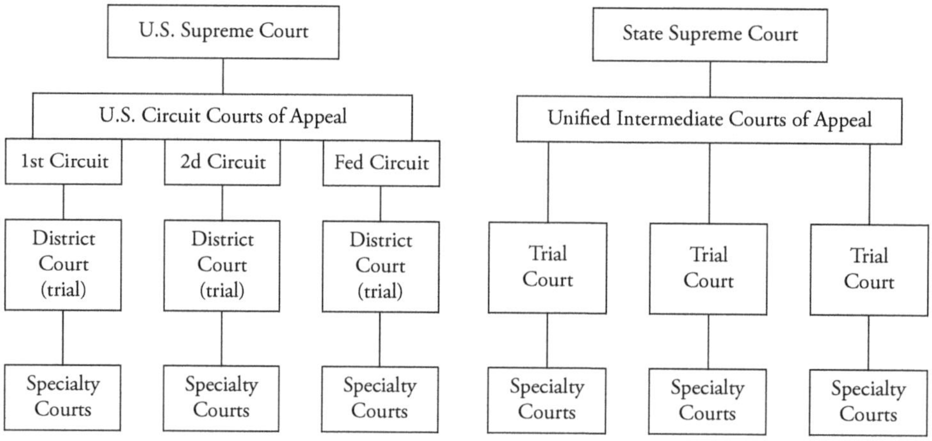

Figure 1.2 Dual Sovereignty in the U.S. Common Law

3. *inquisitorial system*: (adjective + noun) constituting or relating to a system of justice in which the judge conducts an inquiry developing the facts of the litigant's case
4. *legal memorandum/"memo"*: (adjective + noun; plural = memoranda): a usually informal written communication; can contain directive, advisory, or informative matter
5. *discovery*: (noun) the usually pretrial disclosure of pertinent facts or documents by one or both parties to a legal action or proceeding
6. *bench trial*: (noun) a trial in which there is no jury and the judge decides the case
7. *jury trial*: (noun) a trial decided by a body of persons sworn to give a verdict on some matter submitted to them

Use one of the concepts above in each of the following sentences:

1. One of the tasks for students in legal writing courses is to develop a ________________ advising a partner in a law firm on the probable outcome of a case.
2. In the United States, a person charged with a crime could be prosecuted under both federal and state law for the same acts because of ________ ________________.
3. In many countries of the world that have an ______________________ ______________, the judge is involved as the case is presented in court, asking questions about the facts of the case.

4. Some people feel that a _____________ trial with a judge making the decisions is better than a _______________ trial because jurors can be too emotional.
5. The U.S. legal system is sometimes characterized as an ____________ ______ because the two parties argue the case without input from the judge.
6. The typical period of ________________, the pretrial time when parties exchange evidence they will present, is three to five months, though this can vary.

3. Jurisdiction and Venue in a Civil Case[70]

Before any court will proceed with the merits[71] of a case, the court first determines whether it has "jurisdiction" (as used in this discussion, the "right" or "requirement") to hear the case. For trial level and specialty courts, three types of jurisdiction must be satisfied: (1) personal jurisdiction, (2) subject matter jurisdiction, and (3) territorial jurisdiction. Additionally, the case must be filed in the appropriate "venue."

a. Personal Jurisdiction

Personal jurisdiction defines the circumstances under which the court has the authority to require the parties in a case to appear before that particular court to address the legal issue(s). In other words, does the court have the power to serve the complaint on the defendant(s)? There is a substantial body of jurisprudence analyzing whether personal jurisdiction is satisfied when a party has only limited interests or contacts within a given jurisdiction, but those intricacies are beyond the scope for this book.[72]

b. Subject Matter Jurisdiction

Subject matter jurisdiction defines the types of cases a court can hear. These requirements are set out in constitutions and statutes. Generally, federal courts hear cases concerned with questions of federal law and state courts hear cases concerned with questions of state law. However, in some instances, a federal court might hear a case addressing state law claims or a state court

---

70. The discussion here follows from the Fig. 1.1 example using a civil case.

71. "Merits" are the substantive legal issues that must be resolved in the case. Bryan A. Garner, *A Dictionary of Modern Legal Usage*, p. 573 (3rd ed. 2011).

72. For more information regarding matters of personal, subject matter, and territorial jurisdiction, as well as venue and other questions about "civil procedure," *see e.g.*, Freer, *supra*, Ch. 4.

might address questions of federal law. Such cases generally arise when the same events (facts) support both a federal claim and a state claim.

A federal court hears cases concerned with the interpretation and application of federal statutes; the constitutionality, under the U.S. Constitution, of a federal or state law; and cases explicitly assigned to the federal courts, such as antitrust issues, patent issues, and admiralty and maritime issues. Any of these types of cases might also include "pendant" claims (related but based on state law), but such state claims cannot be the principal claims in the case.

There are circumstances, though, when a federal court can hear claims solely based on state law. When all of the opposing parties in a given case are citizens of different states or when one party is a U.S. citizen and the other party is a citizen of a foreign country or is a foreign country, federal courts can hear cases addressing solely questions of state law because there is "diversity jurisdiction."[73] Additionally, for diversity jurisdiction to apply, the amount in dispute between the parties must exceed a statutorily set dollar amount.[74] A plaintiff can choose to file the case originally in the federal court when the diversity jurisdiction requirements would be satisfied. However, when a plaintiff files a case in a state court, but a federal court could have diversity jurisdiction, the defendant can petition to "remove" the case to the appropriate federal court. This is referred to as "removal jurisdiction."[75]

State courts, pursuant to that state's constitutions and statutes,[76] can hear any case addressing questions of state law and cases that address questions of both state and federal law, unless the states are "preempted" by federal law from hearing a particular issue (for example, federal law preempts states from hearing patent cases).

c. Territorial Jurisdiction

Territorial jurisdiction defines the geographic area in which disputes must arise for a particular court to hear the case. Each state is its own jurisdiction and has its own court system. Although the federal jurisdiction geographically includes the entire 50 states plus the U.S. territories, it is divided into

---

73. Complete diversity must exist among the parties. Thus, if there are four plaintiffs and ten defendants, none of the plaintiffs can be citizens of any jurisdiction in which any defendant is a citizen. 28 U.S.C.A. § 1332 (West 2023).

74. That amount is currently set at $75,000 but could be changed by Congress at any time. 28 U.S.C.A. § 1332 (West 2023).

75. For a more detailed discussion about removal jurisdiction, *see* Freer, *supra*, Ch. 4 § 4.8.

76. For example, some states have trial level courts that can hear only civil cases and misdemeanor criminal cases, while other courts in that state could hear civil cases and all types of criminal cases, both misdemeanor and felony cases.

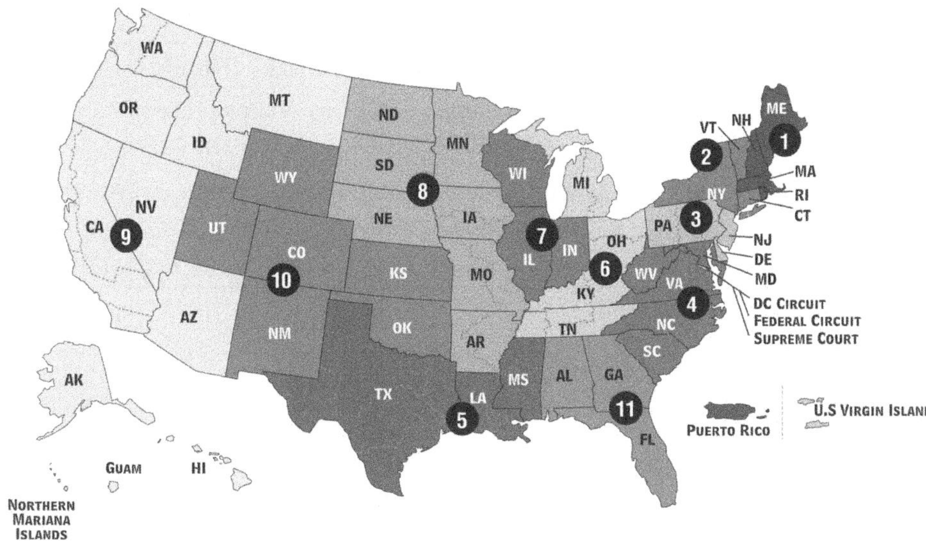

Figure 1.3 Geographic Boundaries for the Federal Judicial Circuits
From https://www.uscourts.gov/sites/default/files/u.s._federal_courts_circuit_map_1.pdf (last visited July 26, 2024).

13 "appellate circuits," with each circuit including specific states and territories. Exceptions apply to this geographic organization for the D.C. Circuit, which hears appeals only from the federal district courts in Washington, D.C., and the Federal Circuit, which hears appeals from specialized federal courts or from claims in which the United States is a party.

Circuit	**States and territories included within the Circuit**
First	Maine, New Hampshire, Massachusetts, Rhode Island, Puerto Rico
Second	Vermont, New York, Connecticut
Third	Pennsylvania, New Jersey, Delaware, U.S. Virgin Islands
Fourth	Maryland, Virginia, West Virginia, North Carolina, South Carolina
Fifth	Texas, Louisiana, Mississippi
Sixth	Tennessee, Kentucky, Ohio, Michigan
Seventh	Wisconsin, Illinois, Indiana
Eighth	Arkansas, Missouri, Iowa, Minnesota, Nebraska, North Dakota, South Dakota

(continued)

(continued)

Circuit	States and territories included within the Circuit
Ninth	Washington (state), Oregon, California, Arizona, Nevada, Idaho, Montana, Alaska, Hawaii, Guam, North Mariana Islands
Tenth	Wyoming, Utah, Colorado, New Mexico, Kansas, Oklahoma
Eleventh	Alabama, Florida, Georgia *(was part of the Fifth Circuit until 1981, and thus still follows some precedent cases from the Fifth Circuit)*
D.C. Circuit	Washington, D.C.
Federal Circuit	Handles appeals from subject matter as defined by statutes

What often causes confusion for students who have not yet had experience working with the dual court systems in the United States is the fact that the federal district and appellate courts are physically located within the various states. However, physical presence within a state does not render the federal courts part of a state's jurisdiction. The following chart uses Georgia as an example.

Federal courts located in Georgia	Courts in the Georgia jurisdiction
The trial level courts within the Eleventh Circuit of the federal jurisdiction: U.S. District Court for the Northern District of Georgia, U.S. District Court for the Middle District of Georgia, U.S. District Court for the Southern District of Georgia, Bankruptcy Court, Tax Court	**The trial level courts within the Georgia jurisdiction** are called the "State Courts" and the "Superior Courts." The Superior Courts can hear any case, while the State Courts can hear any cases except felony cases and family law cases (e.g., divorces, child custody). Each county within the state has both types of these courts. (A county is a governmental subdivision within a state.)
The intermediate level appellate court within this circuit of the federal jurisdiction: U.S. Court of Appeals for the Eleventh Circuit (Atlanta is the "home" location for the "11th Circuit" court, but the court also has locations in Alabama and Florida, because these are the other states in this circuit)	**The intermediate level appellate court in Georgia** is the Georgia Court of Appeals. Its "home base" is in Atlanta, which is the capital of the state, but the judges often hear cases in cities and towns throughout the state.
The U.S. Supreme Court, the highest level appellate court in the federal jurisdiction, is located in Washington, D.C.	**The Supreme Court in Georgia** is also located in Atlanta. The justices occasionally will hear cases in another city within the state.

d. Venue

Venue means simply the place where the events giving rise to the lawsuit took place.[77] This criterion defines the particular court within the territorial jurisdiction in which the plaintiff must file the complaint. For example, if Mrs. Smith sues Mr. Jones for injuries from an automobile accident that he caused and that happened in Fulton County, Georgia, then she would file her complaint in a state court in Fulton County, Georgia, rather than a state court in any other county, assuming both Mrs. Smith and Mr. Jones were citizens of Georgia.[78]

e. Initiating a Case in Court

In all civil (non-criminal) cases, the party initiating the lawsuit, the plaintiff, files a complaint. The complaint must first include explicit allegations[79] to support the correctness of venue and all three types of jurisdiction (personal, subject matter, and territorial). For many cases, no controversies exist about jurisdiction and venue. However, in some cases, key issues arise regarding whether one or more types of jurisdiction, or the venue, are correct for the court in which the case was filed. Such issues must be resolved by the court before the court decides the merits of the case, because if the case has been filed in the wrong court, any decision on the merits could be unenforceable. However, if a defendant does not challenge these jurisdictional or venue allegations at the start of the case, usually before filing the answer, and then waits until much later in the timeline of events, the court will often decide

---

77. Freer, *supra*, Ch. 5 for a detailed discussion regarding venue.

78. If, for example, Mr. Jones was a citizen of North Carolina and had merely been visiting in Georgia, then Mrs. Smith would also have the option to file her case in a federal court located in Georgia, or Mr. Jones could petition the state court to remove the case to federal court in Georgia.

79. The complaint and the answer together are called "pleadings." Swanegan, *supra*, Ch. 17 § II.B, pp. 493–94. The statements in a complaint are called "allegations" because at this point, they have not been admitted as evidence under oath, and thus are not yet "the facts at issue." An exception to this occurs if a plaintiff files a "verified" complaint, which is a complaint in which the plaintiff swears to the truth of the allegations, demonstrating to a court that the plaintiff has investigated the allegations and found them to be of substance, to the best of the plaintiff's knowledge. In contrast, in a criminal case, the State (usually a prosecutor or district attorney) brings charges against a defendant, and it is then the State that has the burden to prove the truth of those charges. *Id.* at 494. In addition, the procedures required for a criminal case are constitutionally based, providing significant rights to the defendant; these procedures are different from the procedures required in a civil (non-criminal) case, *id.*, and thus are not addressed in this text.

the defendant has "waived" his rights to challenge the faulty jurisdiction or venue, or to challenge the verdict or judgment in the case.[80]

In addition to the allegations of proper jurisdiction and venue, a plaintiff must also include allegations describing the events resulting in the claim or claims for which the plaintiff seeks damages.[81] In response, the defendant would file an answer, if not challenging jurisdiction or venue. It is these pleadings—the complaint and the answer—that define the scope of the issues to be adjudicated.[82]

4. Additional Threshold Requirements for a Court to Hear a Case[83]

In addition to the existence of an actual controversy and the satisfaction of the jurisdictional and venue requirements, the parties in a civil case must also ensure that the following requirements are satisfied before a court will hear a case:

- **Standing**—the parties to the case must have a cognizable (i.e., monetary or property) interest in the litigation.
- **Mootness**—the dispute cannot have been resolved, nor can the circumstances have changed to render the controversy non-existent.
- **Ripeness**—the controversy must be current, and it must have immediate, rather than hypothetical or anticipated, effects on the parties.
- **No political questions**—courts will not address disputes between the legislative and executive branches of government that are merely political in nature.
- **Exhaustion**—the parties must have satisfied any and all statutory and/or regulatory requirements to resolve a legal issue prior to filing a lawsuit. This requirement typically applies to matters for which administrative agencies have the authority to resolve, although there may also be non-agency situations in which such requirements apply, such as by agreement among the parties in a contract.
- **Finality**—in the instance of an appeal, the matter to be reviewed by the appellate court must be a final decision by the lower court.

---

80. Fed. R. Civ. P. 12(h)(1) (A party waives any defense for lack of personal jurisdiction or lack of venue by failing to include it in a responsive pleading, or by failing to include it in any other pre-answer motion that may have been filed).

81. Swanegan, *supra,* Ch. 17 § II.B, pp. 493–94.

82. *Id.*

83. Jaeger-Fine, *supra,* Ch. III, § C.1.d-e.

C. *Stare Decisis* and Precedent

Stare decisis translates literally to "let it [the prior decision] stand."[84] It refers to the common law's reliance on "precedent" cases to decide future cases. A "precedent case" is an earlier court decision in a particular jurisdiction from a higher (appellate level) court and that addresses the same legal question currently before a court.[85]

1. Precedent Explained

A case must satisfy three requirements to be considered a "precedent" case. These requirements ensure that the earlier case would "bind" the lower court(s) in the jurisdiction, meaning that the lower courts **must** apply the law and the reasoning from the precedent case to the facts and issue in the pending case.

- The earlier case must come from the same jurisdiction—within the state or within the particular federal circuit—in which the case at issue is being heard **AND**
- The earlier case must come from a higher-level court within that jurisdiction **AND**
- The earlier case must address the same legal issue as the case currently pending.[86]

Once a higher court has decided a case in a certain way, future cases in that jurisdiction addressing the same legal issue—and with similar legally relevant facts—should be decided the same way. This gives the common law predictability. When the facts of that later case are materially different (different in a legally significant way) from the precedent case(s), the result would be different; however, this different result has not overruled or ignored the precedent because the court would have applied the same legal rule; it is the different

---

84. Swanegan, *supra*, Ch. 1 § II.C.1.c, pp. 10–11; Fine, *supra*, Ch. 1 § F; Ginsburg, *supra*, Part I § A.1.c.

85. The term *stare decisis* should not be confused with the term *res judicata. Res judicata* translates to mean "the matter is settled." While *stare decisis* applies to a case's potential impact on future decisions affecting the legal rule at issue, *res judicata* impacts **only** the resolution of the case between the two parties in that case. Ginsburg, *supra*, Part I, A.1.d, pp. 7–8.

86. When legally relevant facts in a client's case are similar to those in a precedent case, then the predicted result for the client's case will be the same as the result in the precedent case. If, however, legally relevant facts differ between the client's case and the precedent case, then the predicted result would be different.

facts that cause the result to be different. Note that a decision from the U.S. Supreme Court or a Circuit Court of Appeals is not binding on any state court *unless* the case resolved a question of federal statutory interpretation or the constitutionality of a state law under the U.S. Constitution.[87]

EXAMPLE: In a case concerning the issue of liability for the tort of trespassing on the property of another.

The legal rule to decide whether Person A has trespassed on the property of Person B requires both (1) a physical presence on the property and (2) an intent by Person B to violate the rights of Person A (the intent to damage A's property).

For example, Phyllis Mosbey has sued Leslie Calloway because Leslie stepped into Phyllis's flowerbeds after tripping on the cracked sidewalk in front of Phyllis's house.

In the jurisdiction where the case of *Mosbey v. Calloway* is being heard, there is one precedent case—*Smith v. Jones*. The *Smith* case relies on the legal rule stated above. The facts in *Smith* indicate that Mr. Jones was angry with Ms. Smith and wanted to get even with her by decorating the trees and shrubs in her yard with toilet paper. He came onto her property and began unrolling the rolls of toilet paper and draping it all over her shrubs and trees. However, Ms. Smith's dog, which was in the house, heard noises from outside and began barking. Ms. Smith looked out of her window, and when she saw what Mr. Jones was doing, she opened the window and yelled at him. He ran away, but Ms. Smith had seen him. She sued him for trespassing on her property. The case was decided on a motion for summary judgment.[88] The *Smith* court's opinion stated that both elements of the legal rule were satisfied because Mr. Jones had the intent to come onto Ms. Smith's property to cause damage, which is a violation of her rights, and Mr. Jones actually did come onto Ms. Smith's property.

Discussion questions: Think about these questions and/or discuss them with a partner.

1. What is the likely result in the *Mosbey v. Calloway* case? Why?
2. What legal rule would the court apply? What are the facts?
3. Were both elements of the rule satisfied, as they were in the *Smith v. Jones* case? Why or why not?

---

87. Jaeger-Fine, *supra,* Ch. IV § E.2.c.

88. A decision based on a motion for summary judgment (MSJ) means that a jury did not decide the case. After "discovery," one party (here, Ms. Smith, the plaintiff) filed a MSJ, which asks the court to rule on the issue based on the evidence gathered during the discovery period.

2. *Precedent Overruled*

Can a legal rule from a precedent case ever be changed? It would seem that the principle of *stare decisis* means that the legal rule itself could never be changed; the courts would be required to follow the same rule forever, and only different facts could lead to different results.

Fortunately, the principle of *stare decisis* does allow for change, **if** there is "good reason." "Good reason" generally occurs when there has been a significant change in circumstances since the precedent was issued or when current legal reasoning demonstrates that earlier reasoning by the court was not sound or can no longer be applied to achieve coherent results.[89]

A lower court might decide not to follow a precedent when it believes that the higher court would not follow its own precedent if the case were before that higher court. However, most judges do not like to be reversed by the higher court in its jurisdiction, and thus the lower court likely would follow the precedent. However, a court might occasionally issue an opinion indicating that it believes the higher court should re-examine the precedent.[90]

A higher court can overrule its own prior decision when it decides that the law must change. Such change can occur for three reasons: (1) the prior decision was poorly reasoned, (2) the application of the prior decision has produced unanticipated and/or undesirable results in cases that were not anticipated when the prior decision was made, and (3) modern conditions now require a different principle or approach to the law.

Note the use of the term "overrule" in the first sentence of the above paragraph. A court "overrules" a decision from an earlier case involving a prior, different controversy; however, it "reverses" a decision of the lower court in

---

89. Fine, *supra*, Ch. 1 § F.7, pp. 14–15. For example, technological advances, such as the internet and social media, have caused the courts to rethink how many of the laws concerning intellectual property should be applied. Similarly, cultural changes have resulted in many courts reevaluating how the laws concerning discrimination should be applied.

90. *See, e.g.*, *United States v. Marcus*, 538 F.3d 97, 102 (2d Cir. 2008) (Sotomayor, J., concurring) (stating that she concurred with the result in the case because the Second Circuit was obligated to follow its precedent that established the test to be used when analyzing an appeal for "plain error," but opining that this precedent should be overruled because it was inconsistent with the reasoning in other circuit courts of appeals).The U.S. Supreme Court granted certiorari and reversed the Second Circuit, agreeing with then–Judge Sotomayor and holding that the plain error analysis test used by the Second Circuit was not appropriate. At the time the Supreme Court heard this case, Judge Sotomayor had become Justice Sotomayor on the U.S. Supreme Court; thus, she took no part in deciding the appeal to the Supreme Court.

the same controversy.[91] For example, a higher court might reverse the lower court in a case when the lower court did not follow precedent. However, if the higher court believed that the lower court's reasons for not following precedent were correct, then the higher court could "affirm" the lower court's decision, but such action would "overrule" the precedent that had been established in the earlier cases.

3. Comparison to Civil Law Jurisdictions—An Example

In civil law jurisdictions, a *stare decisis* system does not exist. Even when a three-stage court system exists in a civil law jurisdiction, decisions of a higher court are not binding for lower courts in the same jurisdiction—in other words, there are no "precedent cases."

In Germany, for example, the Constitution of the Federal Republic of Germany ("Grundgesetz") provides in paragraph 1 of Art. 97[92] that judges are independent; they are not bound by a higher court's decision. Instead, the judges decide cases independently, depending on their own view on the law that applies.

However, there is a de facto *stare decisis* system that results in some decisions as binding. Because all civil law jurisdictions strive for a reliable court system that delivers consistent court decisions, higher courts would **reverse** lower courts' decisions when they differ from the consolidated legal opinion of the higher courts. The higher courts, being the last stage of review on an issue, are tasked to state what the law is. For this reason, higher court decisions could be classified as de facto *precedents*, thus binding on lower courts.

Moreover, in civil law jurisdictions, the concept of *overruling* is common. A higher court can *overrule* its own prior decision when circumstances have occurred that made it necessary to change the applicable law.

D. Holding versus Dicta[93]

A "holding" is "[t]hat portion of a court's opinion that answers the legal question raised by the facts of the controversy before [the court]."[94] It is generally considered to include the result (affirmed or reversed), the legal rule applied to decide the issue, and the court's reasoning necessary to resolve the issue in

---

91. *See* Hanks, *supra,* Ch. 1 § F.1.

92. Art. 97 paragraph 1 of the German Constitution states: "Judges are independent and subject only to the law."

93. The Latin terms are *ratio decidendi* for "holding" and *obiter dicta* for "dicta." For more detailed information about the holding, *see infra* Ch. 3, p. 147–48.

94. Fine, *supra,* Ch. II § C, p. 39; *see also Fine, supra,* Ch. VIII, § B.1, p. 80 (Table).

a case.[95] The holding from a precedent case is what actually "binds" a court in a future case, while dicta are only persuasive.[96]

In contrast, "dicta" (the singular is "dictum") are the court's statements that are not necessary to resolve or explain the outcome in the case,[97] although such statements might be helpful to understand the breadth or narrowness of the holding. For example, the dicta might include hypothetical situations that are not at issue with the facts given in the case; however, by looking at these hypotheticals, lawyers can understand how far the facts could differ before a different result would be required.

The reason for this difference between holding and dicta results from the court's ability to decide **only** those issues presented by the parties, based on the actual events that led up to that issue. The court cannot issue judgments based on hypothetical facts or possible future events, although sometimes the use of such facts helps to clarify the court's reasoning as it applies to the given facts in the case.[98]

While this distinction may seem straightforward in the abstract, in practice, as well as in scholarship, the line between "holding" and "dicta" is not a settled matter and is frequently debated.[99] In fact, the line often changes over time. For example, although material might be dictum when a case is decided, at a future time, a new case might come before the court in which the facts are virtually identical to the hypothetical facts discussed in the dictum of the earlier case. In this situation, an attorney might argue that the

---

95. Fine, *supra,* Ch. II § C, p. 39; Ginsburg, *supra,* Part II § A.2, pp. 153–54.

96. Fine, *supra,* Ch. II § C, p. 39. However, a precedent case is not divided into a "binding part" and a "persuasive part" even if the case includes dicta as well as holding. Refer to the discussion above about "precedent," *supra,* section C.

97. Ginsburg, *supra,* Part II § A.2, pp. 127–28; *see also* https://www.law.cornell.edu/wex/dicta (Dicta is short for the Latin phrase *obiter dictum,* meaning "something said in passing.") (last visited July 26, 2024).

98. *Id.*

99. *See, e.g.,* Louis Fisher, *The Staying Power of Erroneous Dicta: From Curtiss-Wright to Zivotofsky,* 31 CONST. COMMENT. 149, 152–59 (2016); Thomas L. Fowler, *Holding, Dictum . . . Whatever,* 25 N.C. CENT. L.J. 139, 147–53 (2003) (examining a line of opinions in North Carolina courts to demonstrate the inconsistent treatment of dicta and holding); David Klein & Neal Devins, *Dicta, Schmicta: Theory Versus Practice in Lower Court Decision Making,* 54 WM. & MARY L. REV. 2021, 2035, 2042, 2048 (2013) (conducting a large empirical study on 13,823 intermediate state and federal court citations and finding that, in practice, the distinction between dicta and holding is "largely irrelevant"); Pierre N. Leval, *Judging Under the Constitution Dicta About Dicta,* 81 N.Y.U. L. REV. 1249–50 (2006) ("The distinction between dictum and holding is more and more frequently disregarded"). For a theoretical approach to this question, *see* Adam B. Badawi & Scott Baker, *Appellate Lawmaking in a Judicial Hierarchy,* 58 J.L. & ECON. 139, 141 (2015).

court should decide the new case by applying the reasoning from that earlier dictum as though it were the holding from the earlier case. In addition to explicitly overruling a precedent, this application of dicta to a future case is another mechanism that allows the law to evolve over time.[100]

Similarly, court decisions in civil law countries contain a *holding* and also sometimes *dicta*. As in a common law jurisdiction, the *holding* is the "binding" part of a decision, while *dicta* are not "binding." Even though the general expectation in a civil law jurisdiction is that judges should decide only about the legal question before the court, based on the facts of the controversy, sometimes the court opinions can include *dicta*. The *dicta* explain the background of the reasoning and some additional information, similar to *dicta* in the common law. However, the parties, as well as others, cannot rely on *dicta* in the future and should not build a legal strategy for a future case solution on it.

E. How Common Law Is Made and How It Evolves

Using the Attractive Nuisance Doctrine, this section briefly illustrates how the courts created a legal rule and how that rule evolved through case law to its current form. The Attractive Nuisance Doctrine provides the legal rule to hold a property owner liable for the death or injury of a child who trespasses onto the owner's land.[101] The original general rule was that a landowner owed no duty to protect a person from harm when that person had trespassed on the landowner's property.[102] However, over time the courts created an exception to recognize that certain trespassers, namely children, might not be responsible for their own injuries under certain conditions.

The U.S. Supreme Court recognized this exception in 1873 in *Sioux City & Pacific Railroad Co. v. Stout*,[103] in which the Court affirmed a jury verdict for the child and held that the landowner (the railroad company) was liable when a child was injured while playing on a railroad turntable (the

---

100. Ginsburg, *supra*, Part II § A.2, pp. 153–54.

101. The current version of the rule is accepted in some form by virtually all jurisdictions in the United States. *See* Restatement (Second) of Torts, § 339 cmt. b. Although the legal rule developed originally through the common law, many states have now adopted the rule through case law (meaning the rule is still a common law rule), while other states have codified it (i.e., the legislative body enacted a statute with the requirements to impose liability).

102. *See* Restatement (Second) of Torts § 520B. This general rule is still followed in the majority of states today. *See Modern Status of Rules Conditioning Landowner's Liability Upon Status of Injured Party as Invitee, Licensee, or Trespasser*, 22 A.L.R.4th 294 (Westlaw originally published in 1983 but updated weekly with relevant new cases).

103. 84 U.S. (17 Wall.) 657, 21 L. Ed. 745 (1873) (cited in Restatement [Second] Torts, § 339 cmt. b).

mechanism that allows a train to change direction). From this case, the early rule was often called the "turntable doctrine."[104] The rule set forth in this case could be stated as follows: The landowner is liable for harm to a trespassing child when the harm is caused by an artificial condition that is inherently dangerous to a young person.[105]

Two years later, the Minnesota Supreme Court decided *Keffe v. Milwaukee & St. Paul Railway Co.*,[106] which also held a railroad company liable for harm to a child injured when playing on the defendant's turntable. In *Keffe*, the court established the premise that the defendant railroad had created the condition that enticed the child onto the property, and thus the defendant was liable. In 1922, the U.S. Supreme Court in *United Zinc & Chemical Co. v. Britt* accepted the requirement that a trespassing child must have been enticed onto the property by the artificial condition.[107] The *Britt* Court found that the children in the case had not been lured onto the property, and thus the Court reversed the judgment for the deceased children's parents.[108] This enticement requirement gained considerable acceptance across the United States in courts where such claims were allowed under the exception to the general rule of no liability for a trespasser.[109] From the *Keffe* and *Britt* cases, the name "attractive nuisance" arose, which is still used as a name for this legal rule in many states today.

Over time, the attractive nuisance doctrine was used to sue other landowners, in addition to just railroads, for artificial conditions in addition to turntables, such as swimming pools and construction sites.[110] Also over time,

104. Restatement (Second) Torts § 339 cmt. b.

105. *Id.*

106. 21 Minn. 207 (1875) (also cited in Restatement [Second] Torts, § 339 cmt. b).

107. 258 U.S. 268, 42 S. Ct. 299, 66 L. Ed. 615, 26 A.L.R. 28 (1922) (also cited in Restatement [Second] Torts, § 339 cmt. b).

108. *Id.*

109. Restatement (Second) Torts § 339 cmt. b.

110. *E.g., Rubio v. Davis*, 500 S.E.2d 367 (Ga. Ct. App. 1998) (reversing the lower court's holding of no liability when there were genuine issues of material fact whether elements of the attractive nuisance rule applied, thus remanding the attractive nuisance issue for trial); *Kessler v. Mortenson*, 16 P.3d 1225 (Utah 2000) (reversing the lower court and holding that the attractive nuisance doctrine could apply in cases of a child's injury on a residential construction site and adopting § 339 of the Restatement [Second] of Torts as the rule for attractive nuisance cases); *Renaud v. Black*, 561 S.E.2d 183 (Ga. Ct. App. 2002) (affirming the lower court's grant of summary judgment to landowners in an attractive nuisance case when some elements of the doctrine were not satisfied); *Fedewa v. Robert Clancy Contracting, Inc.*, 2008 WL 509848, 2008 Mich App. LEXIS 413 (Mich. App. Feb. 26, 2008) (reversing summary judgment for defendant when there were genuine issues of material fact regarding whether the deceased child was a trespasser and whether the construction sand pile was an attractive nuisance), *appeal dismissed*, 482 Mich. 948 (2008).

the law evolved in both federal and state courts away from the concepts of strict liability to impose liability more in line with general principles of negligence. Thus, the more modern version of the rule imposes liability on a landowner for harm to trespassing children caused by an artificial condition when (1) the location of the condition is a place where the landowner "knows or has reason to know children are likely to trespass"; (2) the condition is one that the owner knows or has reason to know "involve[s] an unreasonable risk of death or serious bodily harm to such children"; (3) the children, because of their youth, do not realize the risk involved; (4) the burden to the landowner to minimize or eliminate the danger and properly maintain the artificial condition is slight compared to the risk to the children; and (5) the landowner "fails to take reasonable care to eliminate the danger or otherwise protect the children."[111] Through this example, you can see how a law in a common law system has evolved over time.

The chart below illustrates the origination and evolution of the Attractive Nuisance Doctrine described in the preceding text.

Prior to 1873	The "original" general rule: A landowner did not owe a duty to protect a person from harm when that person was trespassing on the land.
1873—*Sioux City & Pacific Railroad Co. v. Stout*, U.S. Supreme Court	Rule from this case: A landowner is liable for harm to a trespassing child caused by an artificial condition on the property when that condition is inherently dangerous to a child.
1875—*Keffe v. Milwaukee & St. Paul Railway Co.*, Minnesota Supreme Court	Rule from this case: A landowner is liable for harm to a trespassing child caused by an artificial condition on the property when that condition is inherently dangerous to a child and that condition enticed the child onto the property.
1922—*United Zinc & Chemical Co. v. Britt*, U.S. Supreme Court	The U.S. Supreme Court adopted the enticement requirement set forth in the *Keffe* case.
After 1922	Over time the law evolved from the strict liability rule described above to the more traditional negligence rule set forth in the text above taken from Restatement (Second) of Torts § 339.

111. Restatement (Second) of Torts, § 339.

Key Concepts 3: The following concepts are significant in understanding the U.S. common law system. Read over the definitions given below and then choose the appropriate concept for each blank in the exercise that follows. Check your answers with the Answer Key.

1. *jurisdiction*: (noun) the limits or territory where the authority to interpret and apply the law may be exercised
2. *venue*: (noun) the place or county in which take place the alleged events from which a legal action arises
3. *precedent*: (noun or adjective) something done or said that may serve as an example or rule to authorize or justify a subsequent act of the same or an analogous kind
4. *overrule*: (verb) to rule against
5. *reverse*: (verb) to overthrow, set aside, or make void a legal decision by a contrary decision
6. *holding*: (noun) a ruling of a court, especially on an issue of law raised in a case
7. *dicta*: (noun, plural; dictum is singular) a judge's expression of opinion on a point other than the precise issue involved in determining a case

Use one of the concepts above in each of the following sentences:

1. An appeals court may ______________ the decision of a lower court by substituting its own decision or sending the case back to the lower court for a new trial.
2. In the American legal system, courts look at _________________, or past court decisions, for guidance when deciding cases.
3. In criminal cases, the proper __________________ is the locale where the crime was committed or, in murder, where the body was found.
4. The judge included _______________, her individual view on the situation, when composing her opinion.
5. The judge __________________ the attorney's objection to the question asked of the witness; so, the witness had to answer the question.
6. If a suit is filed in a place where the court does not have ____________ over the case, the suit may be dismissed.
7. In a case including several legal issues, a court's opinion will include the ___________________ for all the issues.

F. Chapter Discussion Questions

Think about these questions and/or discuss them with a partner.

1. What terms have we studied that would describe the court system in your country (common law, civil code, adversarial, inquisitorial, etc.)?
2. What are the three branches of government in the United States? What is each branch responsible for? How are these similar to or different from the government in your country?
3. Give an example of a "check and balance" that one branch of the U.S. government has on another branch.
4. What are the three main types of cases typically heard by a court?
5. What are the three main types of jurisdiction a court must have to hear a case?
6. What are the additional threshold requirements for a court to hear a case?
7. Does the judicial branch of government have the authority to decide the constitutionality of a law, regardless of whether that law is a statute, a common law rule, or an agency regulation?
8. What are the requirements for a case to be considered a precedent?
9. When can a precedent be overruled? How might this happen?
10. What is the difference between "holding" and "dicta"?
11. What teaching methods characterized your law school classes? Did you professors use the Socratic Method at all?
12. What do you think are the benefits and challenges of using the Socratic Method to teach law?

Chapter 2
Sources of Legal Authority and Researching Law

A. Legal Information, Legal Authority, and Legal Advice

Legal information is all around us—on television and radio; in blogposts and other social media; in newspapers, magazines, journals, and books. However, not all legal information is "legal authority." The term "legal authority" can be viewed either narrowly or broadly. Looked at narrowly, "legal authority" refers only to "the law"—what is described below as "primary authority." In a broader sense, the term "legal authority" encompasses the actual law along with a select array of materials that explain, discuss, or analyze the law, which are described below as secondary authority.

Lawyers in the United States use both primary and secondary authority to find and evaluate the laws needed to answer a client's legal questions and to provide that client with legal advice—drawing conclusions regarding how the laws apply to a client's factual situation and recommending options and strategies the client should consider in resolving those legal questions. Section B below describes the types of primary and secondary authorities. Section C provides a brief overview of the purpose and form for legal citation in the United States, and section D provides a brief overview of the research process in U.S. common law.

B. Sources of Legal Authority in the U.S. Common Law System

In the American common law system, there are two types of legal authority: primary authority and secondary authority.

1. Primary Authority

Primary authority ***IS*** the law. It can be either "binding" (mandatory) or "persuasive." Primary authority is binding when it is the law from the jurisdiction in which the client's pending legal issue must be decided. However, as discussed below in section C, there are circumstances when primary authority might be only persuasive. There are four sources of primary authority: constitutions, statutes, regulations, and cases.

a. Constitutions

The supreme law in the United States is the U.S. Constitution.[1] All laws, both federal and state, must adhere to the principles and rights set forth in the U.S. Constitution and the Amendments, including the Bill of Rights, which is the name given to the first ten amendments to the Constitution. Additionally, each state has its own constitution, which can grant broader rights than those in the U.S. Constitution but cannot restrict or limit any of the rights granted by the U.S. Constitution.

b. Statutes

Federal law in the United States is governed virtually entirely by statutes and regulations; there is no federal "common law." The full complement of federal statutes is defined in the "United States Code" (U.S.C.), which is divided into 54 "titles," such as Aliens & Nationality, Commerce & Trade, Copyrights, and Labor, for example.[2]

Each state enacts its own statutes.[3] Each state's statutory scheme is different, and although the federal and all of the states' statutes address the same

---

1. To view the U.S. Constitution, go to the FindLaw website at http://constitution.findlaw.com (last viewed February 2, 2024).

2. To access the U.S. code, as well as all publicly available documents, go to the website for the federal Government Printing Office at https://www.govinfo.gov (last viewed February 2, 2024). The titles and statutes in the U.S. Code can be browsed at the FindLaw website at http://codes.lp.findlaw.com/uscode (last viewed February 2, 2024).

3. To access and browse the statutes from various states, go to the FindLaw website at http://codes.findlaw.com (last viewed February 2, 2024), and click on the link for the particular state. In addition, in the state section, its constitution, its regulations, and its case law can be accessed.

substantive areas of law (for example, torts, criminal law, contracts), the statutory language can vary among the states and between each state and the federal government.

Although many of the statutes in these various jurisdictions—both state and federal—address the same legal rights and behaviors, the federal government and each state is a separate "sovereign," and thus some claims could be asserted under both federal and state law for the same actions, or failure to act. For example, employment discrimination is most often filed as a federal civil claim under federal law (Title VII of the Civil Rights Act), but many states also have statutes providing remedies for employment discrimination.[4]

c. Regulations

The regulations (or "rules," as they are sometimes called) are enacted by the agencies within the executive branch of government. These regulations provide detailed guidance to the public concerning the requirements for the day-to-day operations of the law. The federal agency regulations are set out in the "Code of Federal Regulations" (C.F.R.), which is also organized by "titles," although the title numbering scheme here does not necessarily correspond to the title numbering scheme within the U.S. Code.[5]

Each state also has regulations enacted by the agencies that are part of the state's executive branch of government.[6]

d. Cases[7]

Cases form the heart of the common law. As described in Chapter 1, what was historically thought of as "the common law" developed through cases. Today, common law legal rules continue to evolve through cases, and even constitutional and statutory law is interpreted through cases. Thus, each court issuing an opinion understands that the opinion is an opportunity to educate

---

4. Even some criminal acts can be prosecuted under both a federal and a state law without giving rise to a claim of "double jeopardy" by a defendant. The term "double jeopardy" generally refers to the bar on a second prosecution after either an acquittal or a conviction for a crime and the prohibition of multiple punishments for the same offense. Definition from the dictionary at FindLaw.com, http://dictionary.findlaw.com/ (last viewed February 2, 2024). *See also* U.S. Const., Amend. V (no person shall "be subject for the same offense to be twice put in jeopardy of life or limb.")

5. For additional information, go to https://www.govinfo.gov/app/collection/fr (last viewed February 2, 2024).

6. To access the regulations for a state, go to the FindLaw website at http://codes.findlaw.com/ (last visited February 2, 2024), and click on the link for the particular state.

7. A "case" may sometimes be called a "case opinion," a "judicial opinion," or an "opinion," although the usual term is simply a "case."

the lawyers in the case, other lawyers, and even the public about the law: how it operates on the facts in a particular case (the holding), how it might affect other factual situations (dicta), and sometimes, the public policy underpinning the law (why the law at issue includes its particular requirements), as well as how that public policy is furthered or undermined by the holding in the case.

The cases are published in "reporters," which are multi-volume sets of opinions organized by date. These reporters may also be specific to a particular level of court. For example, federal court cases are published as follows: cases from the U.S. District Courts (the trial level courts) are published in the Federal Supplement Reporter or the Federal Rules Decisions Reporter; cases from the U.S. Circuit Courts of Appeals (the intermediate appellate level courts) are published in the Federal Reporter; cases from the U.S. Supreme Court are published in the U.S. Reporter and in the Supreme Court Reporter.[8]

Cases from each state are available through "regional reporters," which include case opinions from several states in a geographic area—for example, cases from the appellate courts in Georgia are included in the South Eastern Reporter, which also includes cases from North Carolina, South Carolina, Virginia, and West Virginia. Sometimes, a state will also publish its cases in "official reporters," which are state-funded publications, and thus include cases only from that state, and then likely only from a specific court. For example, cases from the Georgia Court of Appeals (the intermediate level appellate court) are included in the Georgia Appeals Reporter, while cases from the Georgia Supreme Court are included in the Georgia Reporter.

The cases in all reporters are organized by the dates the case was published, and each reporter volume includes cases issued during the same time period, resulting in many, many volumes for each reporter. Thus, the Federal Supplement, Federal, and the U.S. reporters, as well as the regional reporters, have been organized into "series"—first, second, third, etc. When the number of volumes in a particular series reaches "999," that series ends, and a new series begins. For example, the earliest federal cases from the circuit courts of

---

8. The Supreme Court Reporter (S.Ct.), the Federal Reporter (F., F.2d, F.3d, F.4th), the Federal Supplement Reporter (F. Supp., F. Supp. 2d), and the Federal Rules Decision (F.R.D.) Reporter are all published by Thomson Reuters (formerly West), while the U.S. Reporter is published by the by the Reporter of Decisions (*see* 28 U.S.C. § 673) through the Government Printing Office.

appeals would be included in the Federal Reporter, First Series (abbreviated "F." in citations); more recent cases were published in the Federal Reporter, Second Series (F.2d), while the most recent cases are now in the Federal Reporter, Third and Fourth Series (R.3d and F.4th).

Because of this organization by date, a legal researcher cannot start research simply by picking up a reporter volume and browsing through the cases. To find a case that addresses a particular legal question, the lawyer must rely on other sources and means, such as the secondary authority described below, to find cases relevant to the legal question at issue. Further, as seen in section D in this chapter, titled "Citations to Legal Authority," the lawyer must make sure to have the correct volume number ***and*** the correct reporter series in the citation to ensure a reader can find the relevant case.

2. Secondary Legal Authority[9]

Introduction

Secondary authority is not itself law, but it discusses or analyzes the law. It is ***never binding***; it is ***always only persuasive***, and the degree of persuasion can vary significantly depending on the type of secondary authority, the author's reputation, the timeliness of the materials, and the depth and/or breadth of the discussion. Thus, even the writings of learned scholars and esteemed practitioners, as well as the non-case writings of judges, are secondary legal authority and are never binding on any court.

Even though it is only persuasive, secondary authority is usually an excellent starting point for research when the lawyer must analyze an issue in an unfamiliar or rapidly changing area of the law. Reading secondary authority can help narrow the focus of the legal issues, provide the necessary legal rules in an easy-to-understand manner, and virtually always lead to primary authority through footnotes or endnotes.

---

9. In civil law jurisdictions, legal scholars and judges are considered experts in the law. Their published manuscripts, articles, and other documents expound on how the law should be interpreted and applied. Swanegan, *supra*, Ch. 1 § II.B, p. 7; Nedzel, *supra*, Ch. 1, § II.B.2. In contrast, in U.S. common law, although many law professors, legal scholars, and eminent practitioners produce highly persuasive analyses and explanations of the law, these materials are nonetheless considered secondary authority and their impact in the legal arena is not as strong as the scholarly writings in a civil law jurisdiction.

The five main categories of secondary authority are described below.

a. Legal Encyclopedias

Legal encyclopedias provide an overview and background about a particular area of law, and thus a legal encyclopedia is very useful when the client's issue is in an area of law not familiar to the attorney. In addition, the footnotes in legal encyclopedias lead to primary sources.

The two main legal encyclopedias in the United States are American Jurisprudence—Second Edition (Am. Jur. 2d) and Corpus Juris Secundum (C.J.S.). Both of these are organized by topics, and the topics are arranged alphabetically; however, the location for a specific claim or defense may differ between the topics in the two encyclopedias. For example, information about the Doctrine of Attractive Nuisance is found in Am. Jur. 2d under the topic "Property," while it is addressed in C.J.S. under the topic "Negligence." Further, even if included under the same topic, the location within the topic might differ between the encyclopedias.

Additionally, both of these encyclopedias cover all the jurisdictions in the United States, so neither encyclopedia might include primary authority for the jurisdiction in which the client's issue arose. However, virtually every state has its own legal encyclopedia, similarly organized, but addressing only the law within the particular state. Thus, when researching an issue of state law, it is preferable, but not necessary, for an attorney to use a state-specific legal encyclopedia when broad information is needed.[10]

b. Treatises

A treatise generally provides a reader with an in-depth analysis about a legal issue or a particular area of law. A well-researched and well-written treatise can provide not only background helpful to understand the context of the legal issue but a deeper analysis and discussion about particular subtopics and sub-issues within an area of law. Treatises can also lead to sources of primary authority, usually through the footnotes or endnotes. Some treatises—those authored/edited by well-respected scholars and/or practitioners—are sometimes cited or quoted in case opinions. The persuasive weight of a treatise depends heavily on its author(s), the historical reputation of the treatise, and its recentness. However, a treatise, like all secondary authority, is **not** primary authority and thus is not the law.

---

10. In some states, these encyclopedias are called "jurisprudences," as in Georgia, where the principle legal encyclopedia is titled, "Georgia Jurisprudence."

c. Legal Periodicals

Legal periodicals cover law reviews, legal journals, and legal newspapers.[11] The articles in these various periodicals can be helpful when the client's issue is in an emerging area of law—an area that does not yet have a significant body of precedent or that is rapidly changing. Many law review articles are often theoretical in nature, and thus these articles likely would not provide appropriate substantive material for legal arguments under current law, even though the law review articles are heavily footnoted.

By contrast, articles in legal journals, and possibly in legal newspapers, address substantive information and practice guidelines for current issues of law, such as the latest changes in the laws within a particular jurisdiction or a recent court opinion modifying existing precedent. Many of the journal articles, and some legal newspaper articles, also include footnotes to primary authority.[12]

d. Restatements

Restatements of the law are a unique category of secondary authority in the American common law. As the common law evolved, it became more and more complex; many scholars and courts believed that the law was thus becoming increasingly difficult to discern from the cases. Thus, in 1923, a group of prominent judges, practicing attorneys, and law professors organized the American Law Institute (ALI) "to present an orderly statement of the general common law within the United States."[13] The ALI developed restatements for many areas of the common law, such as agency, conflict of laws, contracts, judgments, and property, to name only a few.[14]

---

11. A law review is a collection of articles, comments, and notes published by the students at a law school. A law review may address a broad array of legal topics, or it may be specific to a single area of law, such as environmental law or human rights. The articles in a law review may be authored by scholars, judges, practitioners, or students. A "legal journal" is the term typically applied to publications by a bar association, such as the *Georgia Bar Journal* or the *ABA Journal of Litigation*. A journal will usually include articles of interest to practicing attorneys. A "legal newspaper" is sometimes published for particular courts or areas within a state to provide legal notices, court calendars, and commentary about significant cases that were recently decided.

12. Unless the lawyer is researching a familiar area of law, legal periodicals would generally not be the first source on which a lawyer should rely. *See* section D, this chapter, *infra.*

13. Restatement of Restitution Introduction at ix (1937).

14. The full list of restatement topics includes: charitable nonprofit organizations; children and the law; American Indian archive; agency; conflict of laws; contracts; employment law; judgments; liability insurance; property; restitution; security and suretyship and guaranty; foreign relations law of the United States; law governing lawyers; law of American Indians; torts, trusts, unfair competition; U.S. law of international commercial and investor-state arbitration; copyright; corporate governance; and consumer contracts.

These restatements were intended to guide federal and state courts in rendering judicial decisions under the common law. While the restatements are considered highly persuasive sources of common law, they ***are not*** primary authority. The legal rules defined and explained in the restatements can become primary authority in a jurisdiction ***only when*** an appellate court adopts the rule, or the legislative body enacts ("codifies") a law stating the requirements set out in the restatement rule.[15]

In addition to providing the common law rules, each restatement includes commentary by members of the ALI expert panel to that restatement's area of law, explanations of factual scenarios illustrating how the law would operate in various actual situations, and "case annotations," which are very short descriptions of cases from state jurisdictions throughout the United States. Thus, like legal encyclopedias and treatises, restatements can be excellent sources to find primary authority.

Many of the restatements have been updated several times over the years as the common law has evolved, and several of the restatements have been subdivided because the area of law has developed specialty areas through the years.[16] Even when the restatement itself is not updated, the lists of case annotations are updated each year through the publication of appendices for each subject area.

e. American Law Reports (ALR)[17]

The ALR is a multi-volume source in which very narrow, specific legal questions are discussed through the use of case annotations from multiple jurisdictions. The compendium of these annotations for each legal question points the reader to primary authority in the various jurisdictions. As a tool when researching a client's legal issue, however, the ALR is seldom a starting point for research unless (1) the client's issue has little or no precedent in the jurisdiction or (2) the lawyer must construct an argument based on the current

---

15. The court or the legislative body could adopt the legal rule exactly as stated in a restatement, or the court/legislature could use that rule as a starting point and adopt or enact a rule with some requirements that differ from the restatement rule.

16. For example, the Restatement for Torts originally had a first and then a second series. When it became time to issue a third series, the torts subject was divided into seven separate restatements: remedies, product liability, liability for physical and emotional harm, intentional torts to persons, liability for economic harm, and concluding provisions. All of these restatements are considered the Restatement (Third) of Torts.

17. The American Law Reports should not be confused with the case reporters, which are the volumes in which court opinions are published. *See* section A.1.d. earlier in this chapter for the discussion about the case reporter system.

trend in the law—for example, what have the majority of jurisdictions decided on this narrow question of law? Under either of those circumstances, it would be necessary to find cases from as many other jurisdictions as have addressed the question.

Key Concepts 4: Primary versus Secondary Authority

For each authority listed, state whether it is primary or secondary authority:

1. statutes ______________________________
2. treatises ______________________________
3. American Law Reports ______________________
4. cases ______________________________
5. legal periodicals ________________________
6. constitutions ___________________________
7. legal encyclopedias ______________________
8. regulations _____________________________
9. restatements ____________________________

Discussion questions: Think about these questions and/or discuss them with a partner.

1. What is the difference between primary and secondary authority?
2. Why is a secondary authority a good place for a lawyer to start doing legal research on a client's case?
3. When are legal encyclopedias most useful to an attorney?
4. When are American Law Reports most useful to an attorney?
5. When can a rule from a restatement become primary authority?

C. Mandatory versus Persuasive Authority

As described above, constitutions, statutes, regulations, and cases are ***always*** primary authority. However, such primary authority can be ***either*** mandatory (binding) or persuasive. Primary authority from a particular jurisdiction is binding within its own jurisdiction but is merely persuasive if used in another jurisdiction.

With cases in particular, cases from the highest court within a jurisdiction are binding on all the lower courts within that jurisdiction. Cases from intermediate appellate courts may be binding on all lower courts in a jurisdiction or may be binding only on the courts within a limited geographical region—such as with cases from the U.S. Circuit Courts of Appeals, where a case will be binding on only the district courts within that Circuit. For example, cases from the U.S. Court of Appeals for the Eleventh Circuit would be binding on all federal district courts from Alabama, Florida, and Georgia, which are in the Eleventh Circuit; however, these cases from the Eleventh Circuit Court would be only persuasive if used by a lawyer to make an argument before the U.S. Court of Appeals for the Sixth Circuit, which includes the federal courts in the states of Tennessee, Kentucky, Ohio, and Michigan.

Cases from a jurisdiction different from the one in which the client's case is pending are only persuasive. Factors affecting the strength of the persuasiveness include the level of the court issuing the opinion, the recentness of the opinion and current trends in the law, whether the relevant part of the case is holding or dictum. and the type of opinion (i.e., is it a majority, concurring, dissenting, or *per curiam* opinion).[18]

Cases from a federal court adjudicating issues of state law are ***not*** binding on the courts from that state, including cases heard by the U.S. Supreme Court, ***unless*** the legal question in such a case was whether the state law was constitutional under the U.S. Constitution.

Key Concepts 5: Binding versus Persuasive Legal Authority

1. The client's case concerns a question of federal law, and it is before the U.S. District Court for the Northern District of Georgia. You find the following cases, all of which address the same federal law at issue in your client's case, and you would like to use them to argue a motion on behalf of your client. For each case below, is it binding or persuasive? Why? If it is persuasive, how strong is its persuasive value?
   - A case from the U.S. Court of Appeals for the Eleventh Circuit?
   - A case from the U.S. Court of Appeals for the Third Circuit?
   - A case from the U.S. Supreme Court?
   - A case from the U.S. District Court for the Northern District of Georgia?
   - A case from the U.S. District Court for the Northern District of Florida?

18. The following definitions are taken from https://www.law.cornell.edu/wex/opinion (last visited July 26, 2024). The "majority opinion" presents the court's decision; it has been joined by more than half of the judges (or justices) deciding the case. A "concurring opinion" is a separate opinion in an appellate case that agrees with the majority's result but had a different rationale to reach that result. A "dissenting opinion" disagrees with the majority's result and most often explains the rationale for that disagreement. A "per curiam" opinion is issued under the name of the court, rather than with the name of the authoring judge; it is often "more of the same" as other precedents and thus may have little precedent value within the jurisdiction.

2. Your client's case concerns a question of Georgia state law, and it is before the Superior Court of Fulton County Georgia (a "superior court" in Georgia is a trial level court). You find the following cases, all of which address the same state law at issue in your client's case, and you would like to use them to argue a motion on behalf of your client. For each case below, is it binding or persuasive? Why? If it is persuasive, how strong is its persuasive value?
   - A case from the Supreme Court of Georgia?
   - A case from the Georgia Court of Appeals?
   - A case from the Superior Court of DeKalb County Georgia?
   - A case from the U.S. District Court for the Northern District of Georgia?
   - A case from the U.S. Supreme Court?

D. Citation to Legal Authority

In the United States, the term "citation" is a reference to a specific legal authority or other source from which the lawyer has developed an idea, paraphrased text, or quoted some text.[19] Both common law and civil code jurisdictions use citations.

In the United States, a citation is required **immediately after** each (1) statement of legal principle, (2) each reference to or description of a legal authority or other source, (3) any idea, thought, or expression derived from a legal authority or other source, and (4) any material quoted from a legal authority or other source. Placement of citations can differ from civil law jurisdictions.

1. Purposes

A citation serves four main purposes in U.S. common law:

- A citation tells the reader where to find the cited source.
- A citation gives credit to those who originated the thoughts, words, and/or ideas used in the legal analysis, and thus avoids any perception of plagiarism (presenting the thoughts, words, ideas as the writer's own).

19. The term "citation" is different from a "quotation." A quotation is material that has been copied verbatim, or with the same, exact words, from its original source (or with only minor alterations or omissions that must be noted in the body of the copied text).

- The information in the citation indicates to the reader the weight and persuasiveness of the source (e.g., the court and year of decision), as well as the type and degree of support (through the use of signals and explanatory parentheticals).[20]
- A citation demonstrates to the reader that the positions are well-researched and well-supported.

These purposes also apply in civil law jurisdictions. For example, in Turkish law, citations give credit to the sources and demonstrate the strength and persuasiveness of the writer's arguments based on those sources.[21]

2. Content and Form

The United States has a "uniform system" of citation, relying on two principal manuals that provide the rules for legal citation: *The Bluebook* and the *ALWD* [Association of Legal Writing Directors] *Guide to Citation.*[22] Both of these manuals provide virtually identical formats for legal citation in law practice.

The older manual, called *The Bluebook*, was originally designed as a system of citation for scholarly writing—writing in treatises, law reviews, and journals. It relies on multiple typeface styles, depending on the source cited, which would be daunting to follow in the actual practice of law. Thus, in *The Bluebook*, the citation rules for practitioners are provided as exceptions to the "regular rules." The practitioner rules are organized in the "bluepages" while the scholarly formats are found in the "whitepages." This can make *The Bluebook* challenging for new users to learn.

The *ALWD Guide to Citation* was developed by practitioners (lawyers and judges) for practitioners and thus avoids many of the complications associated with learning so many "exceptions to the rules" for scholarly writing. The

20. Most citations do not rely on any "signal," meaning that the citation provides the strongest support for the text statement. However, a starting signal can indicate, for example, the statement is an inference drawn from the source (*see*), an example of several sources showing the same support (*e.g.*), the opposite of what the source provided (*contra*), the cited source provides background information about what is stated in the text (*see generally*). A brief parenthetical explanation can be provided to offer a description or reason for the signal, for example, the basis for the inference when a *see* signal has been used.

21. Veysel Dinler, *Hukuk Yazininda Atif Sisteminin Standartlaşmasi: Bir Firsat ve Öneri Olarak TÜHAS, Ankara Barosu Dergisi* 347 (2024). Translation: Veysel Dinler, *Standardization of the Citation Styles in Legal Studies: TÜHAS as an Opportunity and a Proposal*, Ankara Bar Association Journal, p. 347 (2024).

22. Some civil law jurisdictions do not rely on a uniform citation system, using instead formats that rely on legal traditions and practices within the jurisdiction.

resulting citations, however, whether from *The Bluebook* or the *ALWD Guide to Citation*, are virtually identical, regardless of which manual is used.

In addition, many jurisdictions, and some courts, have their own "local rules" for citation format, so a lawyer practicing in a given jurisdiction should become familiar with those local citation rules to avoid having a court reject a pleading or brief for failure to follow those rules.

a. Basic Content in Citations

The basic information found in all citations includes the name of the source, the location of the source, the author of the source, and the date the source was issued, which is the information needed to find the source if the person reading the document wants to do so.

Of course, this information takes on a different format depending on which legal authority is cited. For example, a citation to a case would include the name of the case, the volume number and reporter series in which the case can be found, the "initial page" (the page number on which the case starts), a "pinpoint page" (the page number within the opinion from which the specific supporting information could be found), the court that issued the opinion, and the year in which the case was decided. For textual materials—such as books and legal articles—the citation would include the name of the author (or authors), the title of the book or the article, the title of the journal or law review when citing an article within such document, the edition (if later than the first edition), the editor or publisher, and the date.

The following section provides examples of several citation formats.

Figure 2.1 Examples of Citation Formats

(1) Case Law

N.Y. Times Co. v. Sullivan, 144 So. 2d 25, 40 (Ala. 1962), rev'd, 376 U.S. 254 (1964).

case name	*reporter info volume no. + initial page no.*	*court & year decided*	*subsequent history: case was reversed by U.S. Supreme Court and that opinion at this cite*

(2a) Federal Statutes

Note: § = symbol that means "section"

42 U.S.C. § 1983 (2024)
Title number code section number year

The U.S. Code is divided into "titles," with each title corresponding to an area of law. For example, Title 15 provides the laws concerning copyrights, Title 29 addresses labor laws, and Title 42 concerns the Public Health and Welfare.

The "official" production of the U.S. Code is abbreviated "U.S.C." There are two other sources often used by attorneys, however. One available through Westlaw, the U.S. Code Annotated (U.S.C.A.) and the other available through Lexis, U.S. Code Service (U.S.C.S.). The code language is identical in all three sources, but the Lexis and Westlaw versions provide case "annotations," brief notes describing cases that have decided issues regarding the code section, which make these versions very helpful for research.

(2b) State Statutes

Note: Each state and territory's code is organized differently. The citation manuals and local citation rules – usually found on the court website for the jurisdiction – include the abbreviations to be used. The local rules sometimes differ from citation manuals such as the Bluebook.

Ga. Code Ann. § 9-11-56 (2024) *This is the form as required in the Bluebook.*

O.C.G.A. § 9-11-56 (2024) *This is what the local rules suggest, and what virtually all lawyers in Georgia use. O.C.G.A. = Official Code of Georgia Annotated.*

E. Overview of the Research Process

Introduction

The ultimate goal in legal research is to find primary mandatory authority that addresses a client's legal questions and supports the legal advice the lawyer gives the client. That primary authority—constitutions, statutes, regulations, and cases—must be from the same jurisdiction in which the client's case arises for it to be "mandatory." This is especially true as the lawyer identifies the legal rule and defines the organizational structure for the legal analysis.

When the legal rule is not settled in the jurisdiction—meaning there is no primary authority in that jurisdiction—primary persuasive authority is required to analyze the client's issue. Such authority would be from a different jurisdiction, but it must address the same legal issue.[23]

Once a client has provided the attorney with the events leading up to seeking legal help, and the attorney has agreed to take the case, the research process would begin. Each legal issue would require its own research plan.

1. Planning

Before merely jumping into a search for "something" to answer the legal questions, a lawyer should first develop a "research plan" to ensure that she knows what exactly she is searching for and how to find that information efficiently. A lawyer does not want to spend valuable time "chasing a rabbit down a hole."[24] Developing a plan will keep the lawyer CALM:

- **C**onfident that research is correct and complete.
- **A**ssured (through following the plan) that the most current authority has been checked.
- **L**ess likely to miss important, relevant authority.
- **M**ore efficient use of time because the research was more focused.

The first step in planning is to identify the legal issue—or issues. Each issue will require a legal rule to resolve it. The research for each issue and rule should be done separately to avoid confusion. When starting research in an unfamiliar area of law, secondary sources will virtually always be the best place to start. Because these authorities provide breadth and depth of discussion about the law, they can provide context and background that help a lawyer to better understand the legal issues involved in the client's case. Moreover,

---

23. When there is no precedent in a jurisdiction (an "issue of first impression"), the lawyers on each side must research the law from other jurisdictions in order to present arguments to the court on how the law at issue should be interpreted. *See, e.g., State v. Newton*, 755 S.E.2d 786 (Ga. 2014) (relying on arguments based on precedents from other jurisdictions to determine whether a defendant entered a building "without authority" when he obtained consent to enter using a false name and identification).

Further, although not favored in some jurisdictions, the use of primary persuasive authority can be helpful in developing analytical points when there are only a few precedents, or if the lawyer finds a case addressing the same legal question as the client's and the case involves strongly similar material facts. However, precious research time should not be spent looking for a "magic case"—i.e., one with virtually identical facts—in jurisdictions outside of the one in which the client's case arises if there are precedents, even if only very few.

24. Apologies to Lewis Carroll, *Alice through the Looking Glass*, and the allusion to Alice's arguably futile following of the Mad Hatter into Wonderland.

those secondary authorities will also provide primary authority, usually in footnotes or endnotes.

Like any plan, a lawyer must know where and how to START, what most of the efforts will entail (the MIDDLE), and, finally, when to END researching. There is no single sequence of steps that is correct for every issue. Depending on the legal issues and the lawyer's existing knowledge of the law about each issue, she might start with a different type of authority and then follow a different sequence through the authorities.

START OF THE SEARCH

Step 1: When starting the research, there are some preliminary questions a lawyer should ask herself to define the scope of the work:

- What are the client's legal question(s)?
- In what jurisdiction is the client's case set?
- What work product must be produced once the research is finished—memo, brief, letter, motion, email?
- How much time has been given for this particular work product—an hour, a few days, a week, or more?
- Are there any limits on the research—for example, use of only print sources but no electronic research?
- If any of the legal questions are in unfamiliar areas of law, what secondary authority might be helpful, if any are known prior to starting the research?

Step 2: Once these preliminary questions are answered, write the plan, even if it is just an abbreviated list of the steps to follow. First, for each legal question, write out a specific "issue statement." Try to be as explicit as possible because this will help the lawyer stay focused while researching each issue and not waste time on issues that are not relevant. Then, generate a list of terms that might be useful when searching the various authorities.[25] Lastly, make a list of which authorities to search, in the order—at least tentatively—of the planned search.

MIDDLE OF THE SEARCH

While performing the actual research, keep a log of the sources reviewed and a brief description of each, even indicating when a source was not helpful. This log is to keep track of your IDEA:

- **I**nformation needed for citations in the analysis, which will
- **D**emonstrate to the readers that the research was comprehensive and relied on current law;

25. These terms likely would be taken from the legal question (e.g., contract breach, trespass, auto accident, burglary, etc.) and could also include a key fact or two related to the claim (e.g., failure to pay, speeding, etc.)

- **E**fficient use of time through
- **A**voiding repetition and trying to research "what if" situations (i.e., things that possibly could have happened but that have no factual support at the time the research is done).

Many electronic search engines provide capabilities[26] to allow keeping such information saved within their systems.

There is no single correct format for such a log; the lawyer should organize the information in a way that is helpful to her. When searching online, avoid merely copying an entire authority, even an entire case, within this log. While such sources can be downloaded onto your computer for future reference, (1) some authorities—especially secondary authorities—are extremely long and can take up considerable computer space when only a small excerpt from such a source is needed and (2) the log should provide a quick reference as to the usefulness of each authority, so only a brief summary of key points should be included describing the source's usefulness—or lack of usefulness.

END OF THE SEARCH

Very often, the most difficult part of research is knowing when to stop. It is very easy to get lulled into a rhythm of success, whether online or in print sources, when finding material helpful to analyze the client's issue. In addition, analyzing each source to determine exactly whether and how it is useful is the more difficult task, so continuing to research is a means to postpone—procrastinate—tackling that analytical task. Moreover, do not become deluded into believing that there is just one single case—the magic case that will answer all of the analytical needs for a legal issue. There is no magic case, and the pursuit of such a case is merely another form of procrastination.

Consider also, that even when the law is found in a statute, regulation, or constitutional provision, the lawyer still needs case precedents that interpret and apply that law to support the legal analysis or argument. Further, a lawyer cannot stop as soon as she finds one or two—or perhaps even five or ten—cases. The lawyer must read, carefully and methodically, many cases to ensure a thorough understanding of the law—especially to understand how the law operates on various fact scenarios—in order to correctly apply the law to the client's facts and provide sound legal advice to the client.

26. For example, both Lexis and Westlaw provide "History" that keeps track of searches and results, as well as features that allow a researcher to save authorities in folders created by the user, along with any notes about those authorities. These history and foldering capabilities can form the basis for a research log.

Further, for all of the primary authority found during the research, the lawyer will need to verify that the law from each authority "is still good law"—in other words, has a statute or regulation been repealed or amended, or has a case been reversed or overruled? The lawyer must take this verification step before she relies on any authority at all; it is best to avoid even beginning a legal analysis only to find out part way through, or at the end, that the law is no longer "good law." This verification is achieved using a "citator." Prior to electronic research capabilities, the verification process was done manually, using a multi-volume set of information called "Shepard's." Today, virtually all research is done electronically, and the two most common search engines—Lexis and Westlaw—each include an electronic citator.[27]

Thus, how to tell when the lawyer should stop—when is the research complete? When the lawyer finds herself in a loop—when the sources all start to refer to each other and/or refer back to the same primary authorities repeatedly—then the research is complete.

a. Example of a Research Plan

Client problem:

Mr. Alonso is a farmer who lives outside of Atlanta, Georgia, on about 250 acres (100 hectares) of land. He grows strawberries, peanuts, and soybeans. He owns a tractor and has several attachments for the tractor—a mower to cut the grass in his yard, a tiller to create the rows in which he plants his crops, and a trailer-type attachment in which he hauls other equipment, tools, or fertilizer around the farm. He also has other types of blades to attach to the tiller so he can weed the fields. In addition, he has numerous tools he uses when he must make repairs to the tractor, the attachments, and the fences on his farm. He keeps the tools in a locked tool chest, which he stores with the tractor and the equipment.

Although there is a barn about 30 feet (9 meters) from his house, Mr. Alonso no longer keeps cattle, so the barn needs a lot of repairs. Hence, Mr. Alonso stores the tractor, the attachments, and the tool chest with all of his tools in a structure that is attached to the barn and that looks like a carport. It has a heavy plastic roof and sides, with a flap in the front that can be zipped closed. The flap allows access to the tools and equipment. The roof, sides, and flap help to protect the equipment and tools from the weather.

---

27. LexisNexis purchased the rights to the Shepard's pre-electronic citator, and its online tool continues to be called "Shepard's." The citator on Westlaw is called "KeyCite." Both of these tools provide direct verification of whether a case has been overruled or reversed and whether a statute has been amended or repealed.

To add security for his tools and equipment, Mr. Alonso surrounds his carport with a chain-link fence that is about 10 feet (3 meters) high. The fence has a gate in front of the carport flap. Mr. Alonso uses a sturdy padlock to lock the gate, and he is the only person who has the key.

A former worker for Mr. Alonso, George Smith, tried to steal some of Mr. Alonso's tools and equipment. Smith cut the padlock and was loading the items into a canvas bag when Mr. Alonso caught him and called the police. Smith was charged with burglary.

Your law firm has now been asked to represent George Smith.

Your boss came to you and asked you to research the burglary law in Georgia. You are a new associate in the law firm, and the only criminal law you know is what you learned in your first year of law school.[28] Thus, you are not sure what the legal rule for burglary requires to convict a defendant (the accused) of a crime; in fact, you are not even sure whether burglary—or any crime—relies on common law legal rules or statutory legal rules.

To create your research plan, first answer the "preliminary questions":

Question	Answers/Considerations
What is/are your client's legal question(s)?	Issue: Is George Smith guilty of burglary? To answer this question, you must first understand what is the legal rule to convict someone of burglary—in other words, what are the elements for the crime of burglary. Once you understand these elements, then you probably will have to perform additional research to understand how the courts have interpreted each element before you can determine whether Mr. Smith's actions satisfy all of these elements. If at least one element cannot be satisfied, then Mr. Smith would not be guilty of burglary.
In what jurisdiction should the research be conducted?	You must research Georgia law since the events occurred in Georgia.[29]

(continued)

28. Remember that in the United States, law school is three years, after a student has received a bachelor's degree in a subject virtually always other than law. Thus, for this example, you have not studied criminal law for two or more years, assuming this firm is your first job after passing the bar exam.

29. This means the research will be conducted in the authorities (primary and secondary) that address the state laws of Georgia. The correct terminology is not "the jurisdiction of the courts of Georgia" or "the federal jurisdiction in the state of Georgia." Refer to the materials in Chapter 1 for a review of the various uses of the term "jurisdiction."

(continued)

Question	Answers/Considerations
What is the work product to be produced?	For purposes of this exercise, assume your supervisor asked you to write a legal memorandum. "In the real world," if your supervisor does not tell you, then you should ask before you begin your research.
How much time is available to submit this work product?	Here again, if your supervisor does not give you a deadline, then you should ask. Depending on what work product is expected, and how much time you have to research the issues and submit your work, your strategies for how and what you research will likely be different.
Are there any limits on the research?	Sometimes, especially for new associates, supervisors will restrict access to electronic research engines until the associate has submitted a research plan, and possibly constructed some possible searches. Also, each firm or agency may also have certain sources (e.g., a favorite treatise, an in-house database) that the supervisor would prefer or require the lawyer to use.
Could secondary authority be helpful?	If—as in this example—the lawyer has not had criminal law in a few years, and has not practiced in this area of law, then the lawyer **definitely** should look first at secondary authority.
If so, what secondary sources could/should be used?	In this situation, the two types of secondary authority to consider first are (1) legal encyclopedias and (2) treatises. Legal encyclopedias—As indicated in the description of this source, the lawyer could use either Am. Jur. 2d or C.J.S.[30] However, the best step is to determine whether there is a legal encyclopedia for the jurisdiction—and in fact, there is one for Georgia, called *Georgia Jurisprudence*. Treatises—In addition, the lawyer would potentially want to locate a treatise to provide a more detailed discussion of burglary in Georgia.

30. It is not necessary to look at both Am. Jur. 2d and C.J.S. because they will provide essentially the same information, although they may cite to different cases.

Question	Answers/Considerations
Any additional considerations?	The lawyer may or may not have any additional considerations, but do not foreclose such questions and/or concerns. Here, for example, one question probably to consider is whether—after reviewing some material from a secondary source (from *Georgia Jurisprudence*, perhaps)—to look in the Georgia code to determine whether the legal rule for burglary is statutory.

The next step to develop the research plan would be to generate some search terms to use for research either online or in print sources. **Search terms that could be used to research Mr. Smith's burglary question**[31]**:** burglary, stealing, theft, tools and equipment, tractor, carport, fence, gate, padlock, locked gate.

Now the lawyer is ready to execute this research plan!

31. At this point in the process, do not rule out any likely terms; the terms here merely provide a start into the research process. As the research progresses, the lawyer will begin to understand better which terms are more relevant and helpful.

Chapter 3
Law School Education in the United States

A. Education Modes

Education throughout many parts of the world share many similarities: a group of students want to study and learn a particular topic with instruction guided by a teacher or professor. However, the modes (processes) through with the learning occurs often vary among and within each country.[1] There is no one, right way to foster learning: different cultures, communities, and schools use methods best suited to their environments.

That said, there are two distinct modes to deliver information to students. One mode, often referred to as "magisterial," focuses on transmitting information and knowledge from the teacher to the students, primarily through lectures by the teacher, although the students are often required to read materials to supplement the lectures. The diagram on page 59 shows this magisterial process by which knowledge is transmitted from the teacher and textbook to the students.

The teacher and textbook embody the knowledge that is to be mastered, or learned. They transmit, or transfer, it to the students, who then learn what they have been given: facts and their application. The goal for the students in this magisterial system is a mastery of the knowledge imparted from the teacher. Success for the students in this mode is frequently dependent on memorization of the material and the students' ability to anticipate what are the "expected" answers to exam questions.

1. See *supra*, text at Ch. 1, fn. 13.

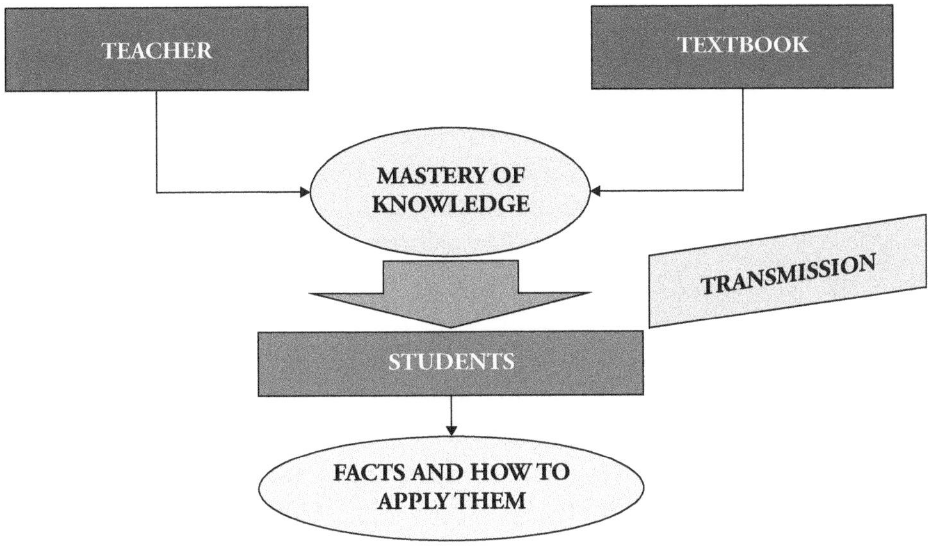

Figure 3.1 Magisterial Mode of Teaching and Learning

The second mode to deliver information to students relies on dialog (discussion) between and among the teacher and the students. In this mode, the teacher is seen as a facilitator of student learning. The students are required to read assigned materials prior to class so they can actively participate in discussions about these materials during class.[2] The diagram on page 60 shows the process through which students acquire knowledge and skills.

The goal for students in this mode is the development of skills discerned through the dialog about the pre-assigned materials. Students acquire these skills by discussing problems, tasks, or legal cases, and, through this discussion with the teacher and other students, acquire the skills they need.[3] These skills can then be synthesized and applied to future situations likely having both similarities and differences from the precise factual situations given in the reading materials (most often cases). Success for the students in this dialog mode depends on the students' abilities to adapt these skills and apply them to the novel situations, as a lawyer would analyze and apply the law to

2. These materials can include cases; excerpts from textbooks, casebooks, or various legal sources; news articles; PowerPoint slides; and notes authored by the professor. The materials are made available to students through various means, including course websites such as Canvas or Blackboard or hardcopies available from the professor or through the university bookstore.

3. In addition to in-class dialog, after-class activities can be employed to continue and reinforce the discussion started in class. In addition to the student seeing the professor during office hours, many course websites provide discussion boards and other interactive tools to facilitate continued discussions.

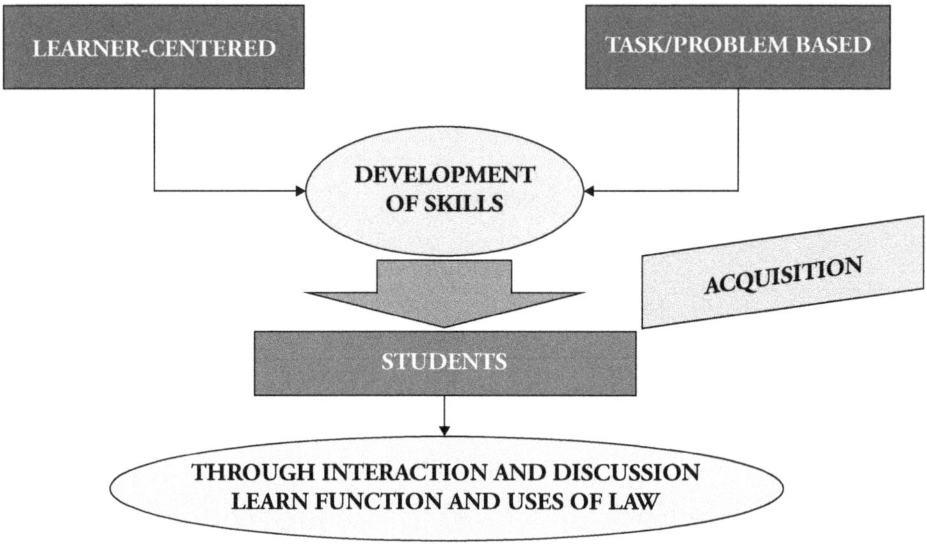

Figure 3.2 Dialog Mode of Teaching and Learning

a client's case. When students are tested, they are usually given a novel legal situation or problem and asked to analyze it and apply the applicable law.

Discussion questions: Think about these questions and/or discuss them with a partner.

1. What education modes have been used in your education system?
2. What education modes have been used in your legal education?
3. How does this education mode prepare you for practicing law?
4. If continuing your legal education means changing to a different education mode, what adjustments do you think you will need to make?

B. Socratic Dialog

This dialog mode is generally called the "Socratic Method," after the famed Greek philosopher Socrates (470–399 BC). He taught his students by questioning them to get at the foundations of their understanding and views—by continually asking questions until a contradiction was exposed, thus requiring them to think more deeply about the robustness of their initial assumptions and understanding of the material. As applied in U.S. law schools, this ongoing stream of questions about the cases assigned for reading in each class is designed to challenge the students' understanding and assumptions about the law, which develops the students' analytical abilities.

In the following paragraphs, we describe the roles and expectations for students and teachers in law classes taught by the Socratic Method. Though not all law school classes in the United States use the Socratic Method, many do use it, and students who understand what is expected of them do better and feel more comfortable in these classes.

1. Student Role

The Socratic Method requires that students be "adult" learners—learners who are goal-oriented and know what they want from their education. Adult learners are highly motivated, not merely passive receptors of information, who actively participate in the learning process through asking and answering questions and drawing on their own life experiences as they assimilate their new knowledge and develop the skills needed for the future.

Students are expected to

- prepare material for classes;
- bring their own background and knowledge to class material;
- learn actively, analyzing and synthesizing material from several sources (their reading prior to class, their professor, their own ideas and those of other students in the class); and
- ask questions when they need clarification or have a different idea.

Because the class is built around a dialog between the students and the professor, students are encouraged to ask questions.

2. Professor Role

The "teacher" in a class taught by Socratic Method is the law school professor. Professors practicing the Socratic Method are "facilitators"—they guide the discussions to help the students realize the strengths and weaknesses of their assumptions and understanding. The professors expect the students to be prepared for class by reading the assigned materials prior to class and by contributing to the discussions. In addition, professors have regular office hours that allow time for students to ask further questions and clarify their knowledge.[4] If a student has a question that is not in the line of the discussion, or will take a significant amount of time to answer, students are encouraged to ask these questions during a professor's office hours.

---

4. *See infra* section B.6, this chapter for more information about student follow-up questions.

Professors are expected to

- facilitate student learning;
- teach about material students read before class;
- be open to student questions;
- be approachable; and
- hold office hours (in person and/or virtual) to see students and answer additional questions.

Professors implement the Socratic Method in different ways. Some may assign students to be "on call" for a particular class, meaning the professor will tell students in advance they likely will call on them during a specific class, so the students on call should make sure to prepare. Other professors may "cold call" on students, meaning the professor could call on any student in any given class.

3. Purpose

The Socratic Method serves two main purposes. First, this method enhances the students' understanding of the cases they read—the facts, the legal issues, and the holdings. Second, this method allows the students to develop their skills to "think like a lawyer"—to identify, analyze, and resolve legal issues by comprehending thoroughly how and why the court in each case reached its decision.

Because students are learning legal analysis and reasoning through the Socratic Method, there are not always "right" answers to questions the professor asks. The professor asks questions to stimulate discussion and examine different responses to legal problems. Students may be timid in answering the professors' questions at first; but through observing and participating in class discussions, students see that all answers have strong and weak points and the purpose of class discussions is to identify these.

Discussion questions: Think about these questions and/or discuss them with a partner.

1. Have you participated in a class that used Socratic Dialog? If yes, what are your impressions of this method of teaching?
2. What do you think the strengths and weaknesses of Socratic Dialog?
3. Why do you think many law classes use the Socratic Method?

4. Preparation and Participation

To prepare for each class, students should read—prior to the class—the cases assigned for the class. As they read, they should keep in mind where the assigned cases fit in the overall scheme of the class,[5] and they should "brief" each case to help them prepare for the class dialog. (More about case content and case briefing in Part C of this chapter.) Also, outside of class, usually in small "study groups," students should practice their analytical skills using "hypos" (hypothetical client factual situations).[6]

In order to prepare for class well, students should read their assigned cases actively, thinking carefully about the legal analysis used in the cases and how the cases fit into their courses. Students should use several different reading strategies. If you do not currently use several different reading strategies, you want to develop the reading strategies listed below. These are the strategies practicing lawyers use when reading a case. There are three main reading strategies[7]:

1. *Linear reading strategies*: skim the case to get a sense of the main idea and how the text is organized. You may want to underline, highlight, or write margin notes to identify, for example, the parties, the legal issues, key facts, and the court's reasoning. This type of categorization can form a basis for "briefing the case" (described in section C in this chapter), which is a more rigorous categorization of the key parts in a case that would complement the following two reading strategies and that would better focus your preparation for class discussion.
2. *Problematizing reading strategies*: contextualize the case (think about where this case is in your class syllabus and how it relates to other cases

---

5. To determine where the assigned cases fit within the area of law for the course, students can use the course syllabus, the table of contents for the textbook, and, if included, the chapter outline provided in the textbook.

6. A "study group" is a self-selecting group of students who work together and support each other as they learn the course material. The group may form early in a semester with students meeting periodically during the semester to discuss the materials covered in classes, or it may form specifically to study for an exam. The study group should consist of a manageable number of students (e.g., two to six students) for ease in maintaining cohesion and productivity. Though you may code-switch among languages if you are in a study group with colleagues who speak your native language, it's important that most of the discussion in a study group is in English: you want to be able to discuss cases in English and use the dialog of a study group to prepare for your exams, which you must write in English.

7. Leah M. Christensen, *Legal Reading and Success in Law School: An Empirical Study*, 30 Seattle U. L. Rev. 603 (2007).

in this section of the syllabus—there are many different cases your professor could choose to have you read—why did they choose this one?). You also want to ask yourself questions while reading the case to figure out the arguments that each party and the court used (i.e., Why didn't the defendant argue . . . ? Why did the court make the point that . . . ?). Finally, as you are reading, you want to make predictions about the outcome of the case; if you try to predict the outcome of a case as you are reading it, you will become more involved, thinking about the arguments and outcome the way a practicing lawyer does.

3. *Evaluative reading strategies*: speculate about the possible arguments; critique arguments made; examine arguments' logic and see if there are any inconsistencies; and think about the implications of the court's opinion. Sometimes using an evaluative reading strategy is described as "talking back to the text" or having a continuous dialog in your head with the case while you are reading it. When using problematizing reading strategies, you are figuring out what the arguments are; when using evaluative reading strategies, you are evaluating those arguments yourself. You want to think about which arguments are strongest, weakest, similar to other arguments, different from other arguments; you also want to think about how you, as a lawyer, would counter a side's arguments.

Many students read cases using only linear reading strategies. However, it is important to use problematizing and evaluative reading strategies to understand the case more fully and to prepare for professors' questions in class. Using problematizing and evaluative reading strategies will help immensely in answering Socratic Dialog questions. By developing your reading strategies, you are learning to read cases the way practicing lawyers do. Developing any new strategy takes some time, but by carefully thinking about your reading strategies and implementing changes in them, you are training yourself to read cases efficiently and effectively, the way a working common law lawyer does.

During classes, students should remember that class is "practice"—not an exam, so they should not fear giving a "wrong answer." There are rarely answers that are 100% right or 100% wrong. A professor uses student answers to teach legal analysis and argumentation, so the professor can use whatever a student says and incorporate it into the on-going discussion. No student can read a professor's mind, so there is no "perfect" answer—as long as a student has carefully read the assigned cases, that student should be able to contribute to the class dialog in some way. If a student does not say anything, some professors interpret this to mean that the student is not prepared for class. Hence, it is a must to do the reading before class and answer the professor's questions as best you can. Learning through the Socratic Method is an educational experience where students are led through legal analysis and professors facilitate this.

5. Dialog Question Categories and Examples

A Socratic Dialog for a case usually begins with relatively easy questions, such as "what are the facts from the case," "what is the legal issue," and "what did the court hold." Once these basics are established, the questions get more thought-provoking, requiring the students to think more deeply about how the court applied the law to the facts and why the law "is what it is" (who or what does the law protect or what behaviors are encouraged or discouraged).

Most of the questions raised will usually fall into the following categories.[8]

Category	**Examples**
Critiquing—thinking critically about the arguments and counterarguments made by each side	What do you think of the [plaintiff's/ defendant's] argument? Do you agree with the argument? Are you convinced by the [plaintiff's/ defendant's] claims?
Commenting—testing the students' understanding of what the court decided	What does the court mean when it says . . . ? Did the court state a broad or a narrow holding? Was this the correct decision? Why or why not?
Evaluating—understanding the court's rationale behind the opinion	Why do you think the court applied this legal rule? Do you agree with the court's analysis that this case is [similar to/different from] . . . ? What is the underlying policy for this result? Are you convinced this is the correct policy to apply here?

(continued)

8. Marta Baffy & Kirsten Schaetzel, *Academic Legal Discourse and Analysis,* Ch. 3, pp. 228–31 (2019).

(continued)

Category	Examples
Applying—challenging the students' assumptions about the holding and/or the governing law	What if the facts were . . . , what would the result be applying this law? Suppose X happened instead of Y, would the court's analysis be different? How?
Comparing—examining the analogies (similarities) and distinction (differences) between the case at issue and precedent cases, and reconciling these comparisons	How is this case similar to . . . ? How is this case different from . . . ? How would you reconcile this case with . . . ?
Speculating—reflecting on the implications of the holding to future cases	What are the consequences if . . . ? Does this case create a slippery slope?[9] Will this case result in a floodgate of future litigation?

6. Follow Up Questions from Students

When students still have questions about materials covered in classes, they should follow up with the professor as soon as it is practicable. For short questions, many professors are available immediately after class to answer questions. For questions requiring more than a short answer, or when a professor is not available immediately after class, students should make use of the professor's office hours. Some professors may require students to make an appointment in advance, while others may have a "drop-in" policy, which reserves certain hours each week and does not require students to make an appointment.

For any of these situations with follow-up questions, however, students should not expect a professor to re-teach the materials. When a student is really struggling, even after talking with the professor, the student should talk with their study group, talk with a teaching assistant or peer tutor, or consult another text or commercial study aid in the area of law.

Discussion questions: Think about these questions and/or discuss them with a partner.

1. In your previous educational system, did you need to prepare for classes before you went to class? If so, how did you prepare?

9. A "slippery slope" is a course of action that leads to a series of events with a final, usually negative, consequence.

2. Of the three reading strategies mentioned (linear, problematizing, evaluative), which do you use? When do you use this strategy?
3. How will your class preparation for a Socratic Method class be the same and different from class preparation you did in the past?
4. What kinds of activities can you do in a study group to prepare you for a Socratic Method class?

C. Cases

Introduction

As described in Chapter 1, common law analysis and argument rely on case precedents. The term "case" is generally used, but the following terms may also be used: "case opinion," "judicial opinion," or "opinion." Looking back at Figure 1.1 from Chapter 1, once a case is decided (either through a trial or motions), the losing side has the right to appeal. After the appropriate notice is filed with the appellate court, that court establishes the schedule for the parties to submit briefs supporting their arguments and sometimes will schedule oral arguments.[10] While the federal trial courts sometimes write opinions, most state trial level courts do not write opinions. Thus, the vast majority of the cases you will read in law school—and rely on in practice—will be cases from appellate courts, either the intermediate courts or the supreme court in each jurisdiction.

The case (the opinion) sets out the court's decision for the issues.[11] The court has three main purposes it hopes to achieve with the case. First, the case provides a written record of the proceedings, which becomes a public record (except under very limited circumstances when the court records might be sealed).[12] A second reason for the opinion is to educate others, both lawyers and the public, about the law—how it was applied to the facts at issue and often why the decision does or does not comport with the policy goals for the law. Third, the case will add to the body of precedent in the jurisdiction by adding a new factual scenario to which the precedent law applies or by distinguishing the new factual scenario from prior precedent cases. In some cases, however, the court may completely overrule existing precedent and establish a "new" precedent.

---

10. Many intermediate level appellate courts allow oral arguments only sparingly, preferring more often to decide the appeal "on the briefs," which is why effective legal writing has become so important.

11. For appellate cases, the issues are those raised on appeal; they might not include all the issues that were decided at the trial level.

12. For example, records might be sealed for national security reasons or for the safety of one or more parties involved.

Cases generally include the same key components, although the presentation of these components may vary, which is especially true when reading older cases in contrast to more modern cases.[13] When reading cases, students should be able to identify and understand these components so they will be prepared to participate in and follow along with the class dialog. In particular, students should be able to identify the issue(s), the legal rule for each issue, the facts relevant to each issue, and the court's reasoning—the how and why it reached the result it did. The case brief is a tool to help you, the student, focus on and understand these key components. The case brief is your tool—it will not be collected or graded by a professor; it is merely to help you comprehend and contribute to the dialog about the case.

After the introduction to case briefing in section 1, below, section 2 provides a description of each case component, along with questions the students should ask themselves as they are reading the case. By addressing each case component separately, even if there is overlap among some of the components, this process will help students organize their thoughts in anticipation of the class dialog. Section 3 then provides an example of a case (edited for this purpose) and a completed template the student could use when briefing a case.[14]

1. Briefing a Case

When reading each case, you should first understand why the professor likely assigned the case. What particular area of the law is being studied, and how does this case fit in with the overall course coverage? You can glean this information by looking at the course syllabus and by looking at the table of contents for the text—where in the overall scheme of assignments does the case fit? This contextual background will help you understand the law as the course progresses, and it will also help you organize your notes when you begin "outlining" to prepare for final exams.[15]

To begin, you should read the full text of the case as provided in the textbook,[16] from start to finish. This will further enhance your contextual

13. *See infra,* pp. 69–71. Remember that the number of cases assigned as reading for each class will vary from class to class, and among different professors.

14. This template is not mandatory in law school classes, and in fact professors will not ask for any written "case brief," but the template can be a useful tool for students as they are learning to read cases in preparation for class dialog.

15. See Appendix B for more information about law school exams.

16. Cases in law school textbooks are usually edited to focus on a particular legal issue or point of law. The student should thoroughly read the material from the textbook and not go off to find the "complete" opinion, as published in legal authority, which likely covers multiple legal issues.

understanding of why this case was assigned—what should you learn from reading the case? Then, you should read the case again and ask yourself the questions below, along with any other questions that come to mind as you read.

As you brief the case, you should avoid merely copying text from the case; you should provide the information "in your own words." This does not mean merely taking each sentence from the case and changing a few words; such action is a virtual copy and does not demonstrate that you truly understand what you have read.[17] You should read a paragraph—or group of paragraphs making a point—and then present that information in your own words, remembering, though, that "legal terms of art"[18] should not be changed.

2. Parts of a Case

There are nine key components in a case opinion. Each is described below, and each is identified in the authors' annotations included on the example case in section 3. In addition, the template shown in the example includes a section for each component.

Caption—includes the names of the parties involved and the citation information. In a civil case, the parties are the "plaintiff"—the party that initiated the lawsuit—and the "defendant"—the party that allegedly caused harm and must respond to the lawsuit. In a criminal case, there is no "plaintiff" *per se*—it is the prosecutor for the jurisdiction who initiates the case, although the case name will often say simply "The State." As discussed in Chapter 2, the citation is the "address" where the opinion can be found.

Procedural History—or the "Prior Proceedings." This section includes the events that happened once the case had been filed in court. Because the student is "telling the story" of how the case has progressed through the court system, that story should start from the beginning—who sued whom and for what claim, or what has the defendant been charged with, if in a criminal case. What was the result of the trial? Were there any post-verdict motions, and if so, what was the result from the motions? Who appealed? If there was

17. Lawyers in the United States believe that if you cannot explain a case or present a legal analysis "in your own words," then the you truly do not understand what you have read.

18. A "term of art" is an expression or phrase that has a "specific, precise meaning in a given specialty." Bryan A. Garner, *A Dictionary of Modern Legal Usage*, at p. 872 (2d ed. 1995). Examples of "legal terms of art" include "contract," "reasonable person," "plaintiff," and "defendant," to name only a very few. However, the term "legal terms of art" is often confused with "legal jargon," (or "legalese"), but they should not be confused. "Legalese" includes terms that merely clutter and distract legal discussion or analysis—such as "heretofore," "hereinafter," "the party of the first part." "One secret of good legal writing is to distinguish rigorously between terms of art and mere jargon." Garner, *supra*, at p. 873.

only one appeal, this is all that's needed for this section of the case brief. **IF** there was a second appeal, then who initiated that second appeal?

Facts—This section includes the events (the details, the facts) that happened before the complaint was filed—what happened to cause the plaintiff to file the lawsuit, or what happened that resulted in the criminal charges against a defendant in a criminal case. The level of detail could vary here—depending on what details the professor expects for the dialog. For example, should the student use the actual names for the parties or merely refer to them as plaintiff and defendant? Are the dates and times of the events needed, would more generalized times be acceptable (such as morning, evening, etc.), or is time relevant at all? Also, when there is more than one issue in the case, some facts could be relevant for one issue but not for another, so the student should make sure to understand which facts are legally relevant, and for which issue, and what facts are merely contextual background.

Legal Issue(s)—Cases in law school textbooks are generally edited to focus on a single issue, but in actual practice, appellate cases usually address multiple issues. The student should identify each legal issue separately because each will have its own legal rule, disposition, and holding. Often, an issue is a result of an alleged "error" by the lower court—for example, improperly allowing or forbidding certain evidence to be introduced, giving or failing to give a particular instruction to the jury, or applying faulty logic to reach a result.

Legal Rule—Each legal issue will have its own legal rule. A legal rule—the law—sets out what must be shown to establish liability in a civil case or to establish guilt in a criminal case. It is like an arithmetic formula that must be solved to determine the value of "x," where "x" is liability or guilt. The legal rule may be a constitutional provision, a statute, a regulation, or a common-law (court-made) rule.

Disposition for Each Issue—This is simply the end result—"affirmed" or "reversed" or "reversed and remanded." No explanation is needed here.

Holding—The holding is more than merely the "result"; it must include the court's reasoning—how and why did the court reach the disposition? This section in particular is where students should work very hard to "use their own words" and not merely copy the court's language. When students put the holding, or result, in their own words, they come to better understand what the court is saying. The holding section should usually include two parts:

1. how did the court explain the law? and
2. how did the court apply the law to the facts of the case?

It is critical that students understand the court's reasoning so they can apply that reasoning to the facts in future cases—in other words, so they can practice law.

The holding for a case can be thought of as "narrow" or "broad." Generally, a narrow holding is one that would apply in future cases only when the facts in that future case are nearly identical to the facts in the present decided case. On the other hand, a broad holding could apply to future cases addressing the same legal issue, with virtually no limit on how far the logic from the holding would reach.

Sometimes an opinion will explicitly include an indication as to whether the holding is narrow or broad. For example, the opinion might include a short paragraph or a footnote describing circumstances when the holding would not apply, which indicates a limit on the facts that could be used to reach the same result as the holding.[19] When no such limitation is included, this usually means the holding could be applied in any future cases with similar relevant facts, even if those facts seem less similar than [OR more removed from] the legally relevant facts relied on by the court. However, even when there is no apparent limit on the holding indicated by the deciding court, a court hearing a subsequent, different case could decide not to extend a holding to the facts in that subsequent case.[20]

Policy—may or may not be addressed in a case. The policy provides the "purpose"—the reason why the law "is what it is." Who or what does the law protect? What behaviors does the law encourage or discourage? Does the law affect the efficient operation of a public body, such as the courts or the legislature? Even if not discussed in a particular case, professors may want to engage in Socratic Dialog about the policy of a legal rule.

Dicta[21]—This is information that can be helpful to understanding the holding but is not necessary to reach the holding. Although many topics may be considered a dictum in a case, the easiest example to understand is the inclusion by the court of hypothetical facts that could result in a different disposition for the issue. Such an example could provide clarity as to the boundaries of the holding (narrow or broad) but would not be necessary to support the holding.[22]

The following is a sample case brief for this case. The authors' annotations are in the boxes.

---

19. A holding could also be narrowed when there is one or more concurring opinions that include limits to the reasoning in the majority opinion in the case. In an extreme case, such narrowing could even preclude the case from use as a precedent in the jurisdiction. *See Riggs v. Highland Hills Apartments, LLC*, 779 S.E.2d 20, 26 (Ga. Ct. App. 2015) (Dillard, J., concurring) (agreeing to the judgment only and stating that as a result, the opinion decides only the issues in the specific case and the case "[cannot] be used as binding precedent").

20. *See, e.g., Old National Villages, LLC v. Lenox Pines, LLC*, 659 S.E.2d 891, 893 (Ga. Ct. App. 2008) (declining to apply the holding from a precedent case to this case because, although the case addressed the same issue, one fact was different).

21. The singular is "dictum."

22. It is often said that if you ask 10 lawyers what the dicta in a case are, you will get 11 or more opinions.

Figure 3.3 Example Case and Case Brief

3. Example Case and Case Brief

Following is an example of a case, which has been edited and annotated by the authors of this book to indicate the parts of a case that have just been described, followed by a sample case brief that a student might prepare for class discussion.

This is the caption of the case. This is a criminal case, so the State is one of the "parties."
Georgia cases are reported in both its "official" reporter and in the regional reporter, here, South Eastern Reports, Second Series.

294 Ga. 767
755 S.E.2d 786
Supreme Court of Georgia.

The STATE
v.

NEWTON.
No. S13G0668.

March 10, 2014.

Opinion

BENHAM, Justice.

The court's opinion begins when you see the name of a judge or a justice (often just a name with a "J.") Some online search engines may include material prior to the actual opinion, such as a summary or headnotes, but such information is written by the search engine editors and is not part of the actual opinion.

***767** We granted the State's petition for a writ of certiorari to consider **a matter of first impression**. As summarized by the Court of Appeals in *Newton v. State,* 319 Ga. App. 494, 736 S.E.2d 752 (2012), the facts are as follows:

A matter of first impression means there is no precedent in the jurisdiction.

Underlined text provides the Procedural History

<u>David Allen Newton was tried by a jury and convicted of burglary</u>, theft by taking, and first degree forgery for taking jewelry while touring a home that he claimed he was interested in purchasing and using a fictitious name on a brokerage agreement. He was sentenced to twenty years for burglary, ten years for theft by taking to run concurrently with the burglary sentence, and ten years for forgery to run consecutively to the burglary sentence. The trial court ordered that upon service of nine years in confinement, Newton could serve the remaining twenty-one years on probation. On appeal,

Newton challenges the sufficiency of the evidence to support his burglary conviction. He does not appeal his conviction for theft by taking or forgery.

Viewed in the light most favorable to the verdict, the evidence showed that a man identifying himself as David Flynn contacted Jessica Harris, a real estate agent in Douglas County, and told her that he was relocating from New Jersey and wanted to look at houses in the $600,000 to ***768** $1,000,000 price range. Harris met with the potential buyer and presented him with a buyer's brokerage agreement, which he signed as David Flynn. He provided a driver's license with his picture and the name David Flynn. They spent two full days looking at houses. At trial, Harris identified the defendant, David Newton, as the potential buyer she had known as David Flynn.

One of the houses they planned to tour was owned by another real estate agent, Cynthia Murphy. Harris testified that the house did not have a lockbox so she called Murphy to let them in. After letting them into her house, Murphy left. While Harris and Newton were upstairs looking at the master bedroom, Harris heard a door shut and ran downstairs. Murphy had returned, and she spoke briefly to Harris while Newton was alone in the master bedroom. Murphy and Harris both went upstairs to look for Newton. Murphy checked a chest in her closet where she kept two boxes of jewelry. She saw that the two boxes were still there, but she did not open them at the time. Harris found her client; they finished touring the house and left. When they got back to her car, Harris saw Newton reach into the back seat where he had stored a canvas tote bag and do something with the bag before getting into her car.

A week to ten days later, Murphy received a call from her managing broker ****788** asking her to check her house for missing items. She checked her jewelry boxes, and they were empty. The value of her missing jewelry was approximately $20,000. Murphy testified that from the time Newton toured her house until she discovered her jewelry was gone, only immediate family members had access to the area where her jewelry was stored.

Shay Brooks with the Douglas County Sheriff's Office investigated the theft from Murphy's home. After obtaining the paperwork Harris had on David Flynn, Brooks determined that the New Jersey license in the name of David Flynn was fake and received information that David Flynn was actually David Newton.

[Text omitted]

***769** After he was convicted, Newton filed motions for new trial. At the hearing on those motions, counsel for Newton argued that the evidence was insufficient to support the burglary conviction because there was no evidence that he entered the house without authority. The trial court denied the motion, noting that Newton never had authority to enter the house because only a person named David Flynn was so authorized.

Despite the fact that Newton engaged in subterfuge to gain permission to enter Murphy's home, the Court of Appeals reversed his burglary conviction, concluding the evidence was insufficient to show that Newton was "without authority" to be in the victim's house. *Newton* at 498, 736 S.E.2d 752. We granted the State's petition for certiorari, posing the following question: "Does a person enter a home 'without authority' when he enters with the consent of the owner, but when that consent was obtained by fraud, deceit, or false pretense? See OCGA § 16–7–1."

Gray highlight is the issue on appeal

Because we have determined the answer to our question to be in the affirmative, the Court of Appeals' decision must be reversed and Newton's conviction reinstated. Our reasons are set forth fully below.

The court's analysis begins below. The court begins to explain the law with the history of Georgia's burglary law.

"At common law burglary was defined as the breaking and entering of a dwelling house at night with the intent to commit a ***770** felony inside that dwelling. Although all modern statutes enlarge the scope of the crime, essentially they vary around this definition." *A Rationale of the Law of Burglary,* 51 Colum. L. Rev. 1009 (1951). See also Anderson, Helen A., *From the Thief in the Night to the Guest Who Stayed Too Long: The Evolution of Burglary in the Shadow of the Common Law,* 45 Ind. L. Rev. 629, 633–635 (2012) (summarizing the historical development of common law burglary from 17th century England through to pre–1960 America and the early legislation of burglary in the states).

Consistent with the early common law, Georgia's pre–1968 statutory law required a "breaking and entering" to establish the crime of burglary. See

Hampton v. State, 145 Ga. App. 642, 244 S.E.2d 594 (1978) ("Formerly, burglary required breaking and ****789** entering. 1933 Code § 26–2401.[1]

[1] Code § 26–2401 of Georgia's 1933 criminal code defined burglary as:

> the breaking and entering into the dwelling, mansion, or storehouse, or other place of business of another, where valuable goods, wares, produce, or any other article of value are contained or stored, with intent to commit a felony or larceny. All outhouses contiguous to or within the curtilage or protection of the mansion or dwelling house shall be considered as parts of the same.
>
> *Floyd v. State,* 207 Ga. App. 275, 279, 427 S.E.2d 605 (1993) (punctuation omitted).

In 1968, the criminal code was amended and Georgia did away with the breaking requirement such that proof of a forced entry was no longer a required element of burglary. See *Brown v. State,* 242 Ga. App. 858(1)(b)(ii), 531 S.E.2d 409 (2000); *Toney v. State,* 225 Ga. App. 228, 483 S.E.2d 627 (1997); *Goins v. State,* 139 Ga. App. 6, 228 S.E.2d 13 (1976). More specifically, the statutory language was changed to require that the entry be "without authority," coupled, of course, with the intent to commit a felony or theft within the dwelling or building of another. See Ga. L.1968, pp. 1249, 1287; 1968 Code § 26–1601.[2]

[2] Code § 26–1601 provided in pertinent part:

> A person commits burglary when, without authority and with intent to commit a felony or theft therein, he enters or remains within the dwelling house of another or any building, vehicle, railroad car, aircraft, watercraft, or other such structure designed for use as the dwelling of another, or enters or remains within any other building or any room or any part thereof.
>
> Ga. L.1968, p. 1287.

In 2007, when the events in this case took place, OCGA § 16–7–1(a) (2007) provided in pertinent part as follows:

> A person commits the offense of burglary when, without authority and with the intent to commit a felony or theft ***771** therein, he enters or

> remains within the dwelling house of another or any building, vehicle, railroad car, watercraft, or other such structure designed for use as the dwelling of another or enters or remains within any other building, railroad car, aircraft, or any room or any part thereof.

In the context of our criminal code and as applied in burglary cases specifically, the term "without authority" has been defined to mean "without legal right or privilege or without permission of a person legally entitled to withhold the right." OCGA § 16–1–3(18); *In the Interest of S.K.,* 289 Ga. App. 672, 675(2), 658 S.E.2d 220 (2008); *Abney v. State,* 240 Ga. App. 280, 281(1), 523 S.E.2d 362 (1999); *Hambrick v. State,* 174 Ga. App. 444, 447(1), 330 S.E.2d 383 (1985).

Until the instant appeal, this Court had never considered whether consent to enter that is procured by fraud, deceit, or trickery constitutes entry "without authority" as contemplated by OCGA § 16–7–1.

Because there is no precedent to answer the issue, the lawyers argued for the interpretation favorable for their side using cases from other jurisdictions that address the same legal rule. Below, the court describes the argument it adopted.

Other jurisdictions which, like Georgia, have done away with the requirement of an actual breaking and adopted similar language requiring entry to be without authority have determined that consent to enter that is given based on a fraud or deceit perpetrated by the defendant is an unauthorized entry for the purposes of a burglary charge. See, e.g., *State v. Abdullah,* 967 A.2d 469, 476 (R.I.2009) (defendant gaining consent to enter by impersonating a pizza delivery man); *People v. Burke,* 937 P.2d 886, 890 (Colo. App.1996) (defendant gaining consent to enter by feigning retrieval of belongings from the marital home occupied by his estranged wife); *State v. Maxwell,* 234 Kan. 393, 396–397, 672 P.2d 590 (1983) (defendant gaining consent to enter by telling the homeowner, who was an antique dealer, that he wanted to discuss a watch); *State v. Lozier,* 375 So.2d 1333, 1337 (La.1979) (defendant gaining consent to enter by impersonating a police officer); *State v. Pierce,* 14 Utah 2d 177, 380 P.2d 725 (1963) (defendants gaining consent to enter by using aliases and forged check).

The approach of these jurisdictions is consistent with the common law theory of "constructive breaking" ****790** where entry in the dwelling is gained by fraud or threat of force rather than gained by actual force. See

12A C.J.S. Burglary § 18; 45 Ind. L. Rev., supra, at 644 ("Most jurisdictions permit 'constructive breaking,' meaning entry gained by artifice, trick, fraud or threat."); *State v. Abdullah,* supra, 967 A.2d at 476 (citing 3 Wayne R. LaFave, *Substantive Criminal Law* § 21.1(a) at 207–08 (2d ed.2003)); ***772** *State v. Maxwell,* 234 Kan. at 396, 672 P.2d 590 (citing to 4 Blackstone's Commentaries on the Laws of England, p. 226 (Christian's 15th Ed.1809) and to 13 Am.Jur.2d Burglary § 13). See also *People v. Burke,* supra, 937 P.2d at 890–891 (citing *Le Mott's Case,* 84 Eng. Rep. 1073 (1650) in which case "defendants tricked the maid into believing they were there to see householder, then entering under false pretenses and robbing house, were adjudged guilty of burglary and hanged").[4]

[4] And see 51 Colum. L. Rev., supra, at fn. 19:

> As to constructive breaking, see, in general, *Commonwealth v. Lowrey,* 158 Mass. 18[, 32 N.E. 940] (1893) (defendant admitted [into a store] by accomplice who had himself fraudulently gained admittance to store [by pretending he wanted to make a purchase]); *State v. Mordecai,* 68 N.C. 207 (1873) (defendant admitted to [closed] store after pretending he wanted to buy goods); *Johnston v. Commonwealth,* 85 Pa. 54 (1877) (defendant admitted to dwelling after stating that he had business to conduct with a resident); *Nichols v. State,* [supra,] . . . (defendant hid in a box shipped in railroad express car).

Like the jurisdictions cited above, we see no meaningful difference between gaining entry by force and gaining consent to enter by artifice:

> The purpose of the burglary statute is to protect against the specific dangers posed by entry into secured premises of intruders bent on crime. The intruder who breaches the barrier with a lie or deception, by pretending to deliver a package or to read a meter, is no less dangerous than his more stealthy cohorts, and nothing in the statute suggests an intent to exempt him from liability.

"Purpose" = Policy; the reason why the court interpreted the law as it did; who or what does the law protect.

People v. Zee, 124 Misc.2d 487, 489, 477 N.Y.S.2d 965 (1984).

The evolution of Georgia's statutory law concerning burglary has been to broaden rather than restrict the parameters within which it may be applied.

Below, the court applies the law (as it explained) to the facts in the case.

Here, the evidence showed Newton staged an elaborate ruse to pose as a potential home buyer. Not only did he use an alias, but he used false identification and gave false information concerning his true identity all to bolster his pretense of being a bona fide potential home buyer. Because Newton's pretense directly targeted the real estate agent rather than the homeowner is of no moment. The real estate agent had a license from the homeowner to consent on the owner's ***773** behalf and grant entry for the limited purpose of showing the home to potential home buyers. Since the realtor's providing consent to enter the home was procured by fraud, Newton's entry into the home was "without authority" under OCGA § 16–7–1. Therefore, the Court of Appeals' decision is reversed, and Newton's conviction for burglary is reinstated.

Judgment reversed.

All the Justices concur.

Citation	State v. Newton, 755 S.E.2d 786 (Ga. 2014).
Procedural History (Who are the parties [plaintiff, defendant? appellee, appellant?]? What happened after the complaint was filed—in other words, how did the case get to this appellate court?)	The defendant was found guilty of burglary, among other charges. He appealed, and the appellate court reversed. The state petitioned for a writ of certiorari (writ of cert), which the supreme court granted. The supreme court heard this appeal from the ruling of the intermediate appellate court.
Facts (What happened before the complaint was filed—in other words, what happened that caused the plaintiff to file the complaint?)	The defendant contacted a real estate agent, saying he wanted to buy an expensive house. He signed an agreement using a false name and provided false identification. The defendant and the realtor toured several homes. Over a week later, the homeowner discovered that jewelry was missing. An investigation discovered that the jewelry went missing when the defendant toured the house. In addition, the investigation discovered that jewelry went missing from another house the defendant toured.

Legal Issue(s) (What has the appellate court been asked; in other words—what error(s) did the appellant assert had been made by the lower court?)	Does a defendant enter a building "without authority" when he gains the authority by fraud or deceit? *Alternative wording—If a defendant gets permission to enter a building by telling lies, is that an entry without authority?*
Legal Rule(s) (Each legal issue will require its own legal rule. What is the rule the court will use to decide the issue?)	A defendant is guilty of burglary when he enters or remains in a building without authority and with the intent to commit a felony or a theft.
Disposition—for each legal issue (Was each issue affirmed, reversed, or remanded? If the issue related to a motion, was that motion granted or denied?)	The Georgia Supreme Court reversed the court of appeals.
Holding & Reasoning for each issue (What was the result & how did the court reach this result? In other words, how did the court apply the legal rule to the facts in the case?)	The issue on appeal was a question of first impression, meaning that the Georgia courts had never addressed the question of whether "without authority" would include obtaining that authority through fraud, deceit, or false pretense, and thus there was no precedent in Georgia for the court to apply. After reviewing the history of the burglary rule in Georgia, the court reviewed case law from other jurisdictions that had the same statutory rule as current Georgia law and whose courts had already considered this question. The Georgia Supreme Court concluded that "without authority" did include gaining authority (gaining permission) by means of fraud, deceit, or false pretense. The court reasoned that including such actions under the umbrella of "without authority" was consistent with the common law theory of "constructive breaking."

(continued)

(continued)

	After deciding this specific question (should "without authority" include fraud, deceit, or false pretense), the court applied this interpretation of the rule to the facts in the case and concluded that the defendant entered the homes without authority. Accordingly, the court reinstated the defendant's conviction.
Policy—if any (Organize by legal issue.)	The purpose of the burglary statute is to protect against the specific dangers posed by entry into secured premises of intruders bent on crime. *In this case, the court explicitly discussed policy (the purpose for the rule as it is).*
Dicta—if any (Address for each issue. "Dicta" = information that is helpful, but not necessary, to reach the result.)	There are no dicta.

Chapter 4
Legal Rhetoric and Legal Writing

Introduction

"Rhetoric" refers to "the study of writing or speaking as a means of communication or persuasion."[1] For centuries, starting in ancient Greece and Rome, rhetoric, along with logic (the mechanics of thought and analysis) and grammar (the mechanics of language), were taught as the "Trivium."[2] Accordingly, legal discourse (all forms of legal writing) has a long and robust history,[3] although rhetoric as a stand-alone subject is no longer taught in U.S. schools today.

To bring "rhetoric" into the current technological world, rhetoric is "the operating system" underpinning argumentation, not merely an app to generate legal arguments.[4] Before addressing how to create effective legal writing, some background about legal writing in the United States is appropriate.

---

1. Merriam-Webster Dictionary, https://www.merriam-webster.com/dictionary/rhetorical (last visited February 2, 2024).

2. Kristen Konrad Tiscione, *Rhetoric for Legal Writers: The Theory and Practice of Analysis and Persuasion,* p. 17 (2nd ed. 2016); Wikipedia, https://en.wikipedia.org/wiki/Trivium (last visited February 2, 2024).

3. "Discourse" is the "formal and orderly[, and often] extended expression of thought on a subject." Merriam-Webster Dictionary, https://www.merriam-webster.com/dictionary/discourse (last visited February 2, 2024).

4. *See* Jennifer Fletcher, *Teaching Arguments: Rhetorical Comprehension, Critique, and Response*, Introduction, p. xvi (2015).

First, rhetorical style varies among cultures. In some cultures, the responsibility is on the reader to understand a document; it is the reader's burden to understand what the writer is saying. If the document does not draw explicit conclusions or make explicit links between ideas, then a reader must work harder to interpret the writer's message.[5] In other cultures, the expected rhetorical style calls for the writer to build up to the conclusion using a slow pace and a gentle or merely suggestive (rather than direct) tone.[6] In contrast, in the United States, the burden for clarity, for the reader to understand what the writer is saying, is on the writer. It is the writer's responsibility to make all their ideas clear and understandable to a reader.

Cultures in which the burden for clarity is on the reader share these characteristics:

- a high level of uncertainty in the writing
- group identity (much shared in-group knowledge)
- indirect communication
- specific application of rules (rules may be specific to a writer or piece)
- nonlinear notions of time[7]

Cultures where the burden for clarity is on the writer share these characteristics:

- a high level of certainty in the writing
- individual identity (little shared in-group knowledge, so everything must be completely explained)
- direct communication
- universal application of rules (rules are the same for all writing)
- linear notions of time (time is presented chronologically)[8]

Legal writing in the United States is reader focused; it places the burden for clarity on the writer. The United States is a culture made up of many different individuals from many different countries and cultures. A writer cannot assume that any knowledge is shared, so the writer must explain all ideas in detail. It is the writer's responsibility to ensure that the text is clear, easy to follow, and concise so the reader has little or no trouble understanding what the writer is trying to convey.

---

5. M. Baffy & K. Schaetzel, *Academic Legal Discourse and Analysis,* Part 1, Ch. 1.B, p. 11.

6. Nadia E. Nedzel, *Legal Reasoning, Research, and Writing for International Graduate Students*, Ch. 8 § I.A, p. 214 (2012).

7. Matthew McCool, *Writing Around the World: A Guide to Writing across Cultures*, Ch.4, p. 60 (2009).

8. *Id.*

In legal writing, writer-responsible writing has been emphasized and enhanced by the "Plain English Movement," which came into focus in 1998 with President Clinton's presidential memorandum directing all federal agencies to use plain language for their written communications.[9] Even though this value for plain language is inherent in U.S. culture, this movement emphasizes the need for government and legal writing, especially, to be easily understood and clear for a reader. Many states now also follow a plain language requirement for laws and regulations. Courts and lawyers also began adopting this plain language style in court documents and judicial opinions.

Discussion questions: Think about these questions and/or discuss them with a partner.

1. In your country/culture, is there a lot of "shared knowledge" in the audiences you write for?
2. In the characteristics listed above for "reader-responsible" and "writer-responsible" cultures (whether the reader or the writer has the burden for making the ideas clear), which are characteristics of writing in your country/culture?
3. In your country/culture, does the reader or the writer have the "burden for clarity" to understand a document? On what basis do you draw this conclusion?

There are several types of legal writing in the United States, which can be categorized broadly as (1) predictive (objective) writing (office legal memoranda), (2) persuasive argument (court briefs), (3) preventive writing (contract drafting), and (4) performance writing (e.g., client letters, opinion letters).[10] This chapter focuses on legal writing generally, and the following chapters will provide more information focused on predictive writing.[11] Thus, the remaining

---

9. Deborah E. Bouchoux, *Aspen Handbook for Legal Writers*, Ch. 4 § B, p. 92–93 (5th ed. 2021). The plain language movement began much earlier than 1998, but it gained momentum with the president's memorandum. It then gained additional impetus with Congress's passage of the Plain Writing Act of 2010 (5 U.S.C. § 301), which defined "plain writing" as "writing that is clear, concise, well-organized, and follows other best practices appropriate to the subject or field and intended audience." Bouchoux, *supra*; *see also* www.plainlanguage.gov/guidelines (last visited February 2, 2024).

10. Linda H. Edwards & Samantha A. Moppett, *Legal Analysis and Writing*, pp. 3–5 (6th ed. 2023).

11. While the overall organization and characteristics described in this chapter also apply to persuasive writing, see Appendix C for a brief discussion providing more information about persuasive legal writing. In addition, although the details concerning preventive and performance writing are beyond the scope of this text, the general principles described in the remainder of this chapter also apply to those two writing categories.

sections in this chapter will describe the general organizational structure and the principal characteristics of effective legal rhetoric in the United States.

A. Organization of the Document

Like all good writing—and all good speeches—tell the reader what you will say (the introduction/background), then tell the reader what you want them to know (the body), and finally tell the reader what you just said (the conclusion). To writers from other cultures, this may seem repetitive and unsophisticated. However, because U.S. readers value clarity and direct communication, this is what they expect in writer-responsible writing. They want to be able to read through a document with ease, noting the main ideas and their support without having to do much work. They want to concentrate on the ideas and support, not on trying to understand what the writer is saying.

There are three main parts to any document: the introduction, the body, and the conclusion. Readers expect the following in each part:

1. Introduction

Remembering that legal writing in the United States is reader focused (the burden for clarity is on the writer), a reader should be able to understand the writer's thesis, conclusions, and logic by reading the document only once. Accordingly, the writer should start by first presenting their thesis—the topic and what the reader intends to prove about that topic. This information is essential to "set the stage" for the body of the document (or analysis/support). If one thinks about a document as the production of a live stage play, then the introduction is the backdrop, or scenery, and the props on the stage—they are not the main focus, but without them, the audience may have no idea what meaning the actions or words of the actors convey.

Thus, by looking at the stage, or reading the introduction, the reader will know, without a doubt, what the writer's topic is and what the writer intends to prove about that topic. In writer-responsible cultures, the introduction provides an overview of the piece of writing, contains an immediate thesis, and tells the reader the main organization of the piece of writing.[12]

2. Body

The body is the "heart" of the document. Here is where the writer provides all of the support for their conclusions about the topic. Providing support means

12. McCool, *supra* at fn. 7, p. 71.

the writer must explicitly spell out the reasoning/logic applied to the facts—the writer cannot assume that the reader knows what the writer intended or how the writer reached any conclusions. Again, if thinking about a legal document as a stage play, all of the actors' dialog must be presented, or for anyone who is scientifically or mathematically inclined and has had to write a "proof," then every step in the experiment or logic for the proof must be explicitly stated for the proof to be complete.

Writers organize their paragraphs by putting one main idea in each paragraph. Each paragraph begins with a "topic sentence" or a "thesis sentence." A topic sentence contains the topic, or main idea, of the paragraph, while a thesis sentence indicates a conclusion that the paragraph will prove. The support for that main idea then follows. Support can be cases, facts, opinions of experts, real-life or hypothetical examples, definitions, etc. Support may contain a brief historical context if that is something a reader needs to understand the topic. Support may also contain a counterargument, which the writer then shows is incorrect. However, most support is focused on proving to the reader that this main idea is correct or acceptable.

3. Conclusion

Finally, the document should end with a "conclusion"—usually a short summary of the key points made in the body of the document. While some may think this all sounds very repetitive, this is the structure that is expected in legal writing, and such repetition has been shown to (1) make the thesis and supporting analysis easier to understand and (2) make the document more convincing, regardless of whether it is an objective or a persuasive document.

Discussion questions: Think about these questions and/or discuss them with a partner.

1. When writing in your country/culture, what do you put in each part?
    a. the introduction
    b. the body
    c. the conclusion
2. In writing in your country/culture, is your main point, or thesis, overtly stated or implied?
3. In writing in your country/culture, how many times do you repeat your main point, or thesis, in your document?

B. Characteristics of Effective (Good) Legal Writing

Introduction

Though there is no exhaustive list of the characteristics of good legal writing, the main goals for an excellent legal document—as well as for all legal communication—is four-fold: (1) the writing must be accurate, (2) the writing must be clear, (3) the writing must be easy to read and understand after reading the document only one time, and (4) the writing must also be concise. This last characteristic—conciseness—often creates great tension with the first three characteristics. While this tension can arise for both native and non-native English speakers, it can be especially difficult for non-native English speakers who are also struggling with cultural differences in rhetoric.[13]

Even though there is no absolute "form" for good writing, these four characteristics generally define what is "good" legal writing in a writer-responsible culture. Developing these characteristics in your writing will help it become easy for your professors, legal colleagues, and judges to understand. When your reader can easily understand what you are saying, they are more likely to give you a good grade or decide a motion in your favor.

1. Effective Characteristics and How to Achieve Them[14]

a. Accuracy

First and foremost, the document must be accurate. If writing about a case, the writer cannot try to fill in factual gaps with assumptions or made-up facts. A writer can use only the known and given facts; they cannot assume facts or knowledge that is not presented. If they are making an argument based on given facts, then they must state every step in the logic of their argument, so that the reader can easily follow their logic and see how they arrived at their conclusion.

If writing a paper for a law school class or an article for a legal journal, the writer must ensure that the logic and support for the conclusions are sound and that sources are cited correctly. All ideas and arguments presented must have some kind of support and that support must be clearly stated. A writer cannot assume that there is any "shared knowledge" between them and their reader; support for ideas is presented and explained.

Also, as a part of being accurate, the writer must pay close attention to word choice and word connotations. This is both the beauty and the difficulty

---

13. *See* text at footnotes 5–6, *supra*, this chapter.

14. *See* Bouchoux, *supra*, Ch. 4, for more information about these goals.

of the English language. English has a lot of words, many of them borrowed from other languages. Because there are so many words, and not always much shared knowledge, writers need to be as precise as possible in choosing the word that best reflects their meaning. For example, look at the different meanings the word "walked" can have if a more precise word is used:

- The man walked into the room.
- The man hobbled into the room.
- The man sauntered into the room.
- The man marched into the room.
- The man tip-toed into the room.

Each of these sentences creates a different picture in a reader's mind just by changing one word.

In addition, look at the following example stating facts in a court brief:

> In Klum's case, the electrical, water, and rat problems threatened the health and safety of his family. The electricity periodically **waned** and **surged**, which destroyed his children's **homework on the computer** and **ruined** his microwave. [Bold added.]

Notice that the writer does not say "the electricity was bad" or "the electricity came and went." The verbs "waned" (dropped down below a minimum standard) and "surged" (rose above a minimum standard) specifically tell the reader what the electricity was doing. This "waning" and "surging" had an effect on Klum's family: it destroyed his children's homework on the computer and ruined his microwave. Again, we have very specific details here so that the reader can know exactly what happened. The problems with the electricity did not destroy all his children's homework, just what they did on the computer. We do not know if this is the majority of the children's homework, but the fact states that this homework, done on the computer, was destroyed. The writer then does not state that "there was a problem with the microwave too" or "the microwave was damaged," but that the microwave was "ruined." It would not work anymore.

Using the precise, correct terms avoids confusing a reader about the writer's intent and purpose. Though the example above is from the facts of a case, using the most accurate words you can find is best in all legal writing. For example, saying a court "ruled," "believed," or "decided" has no legal meaning; the issue would be what facts did the court "find" or what legal conclusion did the court "hold." Then, the court would "explain" or "describe" its reasoning. (Note that a court does not "argue" or "contend"; the lawyers do this.)

In addition, one concept to keep in mind when trying to make your writing as precise as possible is to avoid vague words and descriptions and use precise details. Several expressions in English that tend to lead to vagueness are: "It is/was," "There is/are," "This is/are." Even within a single paragraph, which should provide context for the topic, a writer's point can be lost using such vague references as "it," "this," and "there." If you find yourself beginning a sentence this way, you may want to double-check that the words you use in the rest of the sentence accurately and precisely describe what you want to say, or you may simply want to revise the wording to avoid these terms.

Further, the writer should be aware of word connotations (different meanings for the same word), which can also confuse the reader—for example, describing a person as "simple" could mean that the person is easy to understand ("Mary was a simple person, using plain language and direct sentences to make her points"), or it could mean the person lacks intellectual ability ("David was simple; he suffered trauma at birth, and thus was developmentally delayed with his speech and his ability to organize his thoughts"). When you are not sure of the meaning or connotation of a word you want to use, you might want to check the word's meaning in a dictionary or a thesaurus.[15]

b. Clarity

Second, the ideas and arguments you present in your writing must be clear to your reader. Clarity, or the property of being "clear," is vital for a reader's ability to understand the document. Using the most accurate words helps with clarity—but clarity is more than choosing accurate words. Clarity also concerns how you present your ideas: how you order them and how you label them. A reader should not be confused about the writer's thesis or support for that thesis, and the reader should be able to easily see the writer's thesis and easily follow the writer's logic/progression through each supporting point. For example, many writers "label" their thesis, identify it for their reader, with a sentence in their introduction like "In this paper, I argue . . . " or "This paper claims that . . . " or "Tom probably cannot bring a successful claim against Mark."

In the same way, writers may "label" their support with phrases like "for example," or they may use enumeration (numbering) for their supporting points to help the reader clearly see how many there are and which one is

15. In addition to the dictionary and thesaurus that are part of your word processing program, you might also consult *The American Heritage Dictionary* (a dictionary of American English) or *Longman's Dictionary of Contemporary English*. For legal terms, you might consult a legal dictionary, such as https://dictionary.findlaw.com. All of these dictionaries are available for free online.

being discussed in each part of the document. In legal writing, in particular, writers usually use thesis sentences to introduce supporting points.[16]

As an example, look at the statement below regarding Klum's case:

> In Klum's case, the electrical, water, and rat problems threatened the health and safety of his family. The electricity periodically waned and surged, which destroyed his children's homework on the computer and ruined his microwave.

Notice that the first sentence here tells the reader what the paragraph will prove. The next sentence begins to present the facts to support the conclusion stated in the first—thesis—sentence.

Clarity additionally requires consistent use of terms, especially for legal terms of art,[17] for party names and references, and for relevant objects and events at issue. This may seem repetitive or boring, but it is very helpful to a reader in clearly understanding the writer's idea, argument, or claim. Legal writing is not creative writing, so using different terms to describe the same thing merely confuses a reader.

Clarity also involves skill and precision when using negative terms; for example, saying an event is "not unlikely" can be more easily understood by saying the event is "probable" or simply just "likely." Moreover, some negative expressions can be wordy, such as "not included" (instead of simply "lacked" or "omitted") and "not the same as" (instead of simply "different from"). Even though many of these expressions may be thought of as sophisticated writing, in U.S. legal writing, it is more important to clearly convey an idea to a reader.

In addition, in the United States, readers have an expectation of how the words in a sentence should be sequenced. That expected sequence is subject first (the noun), followed by the verb, followed by the object.[18] Although some variations in this structure can be appropriate in certain circumstances, variations often result in longer, awkwardly worded sentences that are difficult to follow and thus interfere with the reader's ability to easily follow the

16. With thesis sentences, a writer may use enumeration (such as "First," "Second," or "Next"), but they generally would not use "For example."

17. A "term of art" is an expression or phrase that has a "specific, precise meaning in a given specialty." Bryan A. Garner, *A Dictionary of Modern Legal Usage*, at p. 883 (3rd ed. 2011). Examples of "legal terms of art" include "contract," "reasonable person," "plaintiff," and "defendant," to name only a very few.

18. Joseph M. Williams and Joseph Bizup, *Style: Lessons in Clarity and Grace*, pp. 28–65 (2014) (referring to this expected sequence as Character + Action).

document. Keeping your wording straightforward (subject + verb + object); using the same terms to refer to the same people, objects, or ideas; and labeling what you are doing are some of the ways to make your writing, your ideas, and your arguments clear to a reader.

c. Readability

A third characteristic, or goal, of good writing is readability. Readability means just what it says: the ability of a reader to read what you have written and understand your meaning. Readability goes hand-in-hand with clarity: it is the way ideas, or items, are ordered in a sentence so that the reader can easily understand what the writer is saying. Readability includes several characteristics, six of which we will mention.

First, one of the most important characteristics of readability is the use of the active voice, which is tied closely to the expected sentence sequence of "subject, verb, object." The action, or meaning, moves through the sentence from left to right, the way we read English: "The dog ate the bone." The doer of the action is listed first in the sentence (the dog) and the action carries through the sentence from left to right (dog + ate + bone). Passive voice is the use of any form of the verb "to be,"—is, are, was, were, has been, have been. In passive voice, the action of the sentence moves from right to left: The bone was eaten by the dog, so the object, what is acted upon, is first in the sentence (the bone) and the meaning of the sentence moves from right to left, the opposite of the way the words are ordered (bone + was eaten + dog).

Using the active voice results in a stronger sentence and it results in a sentence that is easier to understand, while using passive voice hides the "actor"—the subject—and virtually always results in longer, and often awkward, sentences. An example of a sentence using passive voice is "The Complaint was filed by the Plaintiff." Changing this to the active voice results in, "The Plaintiff filed the Complaint," which is more straightforward and easier to understand.

Second, closely related to the use of active voice is keeping the subject and verb close together in a sentence. This makes it easy for a reader to see who is doing what to whom. A separation between the subject and the verb can occur when the writer attempts to include several modifiers or a non-restrictive clause following the noun. For example, "The defendant, who was found liable for trespassing, apologized to the plaintiff right after the jury rendered its verdict." The subject is "the defendant" and the verb is "apologized," and they are separated by six words. Also note that the non-restrictive clause uses passive voice: "was found." The writer could make these ideas easier for a reader to understand by creating two sentences: "The jury found the defendant liable for trespassing. He apologized to the plaintiff right after the jury rendered its verdict." Another way to make these ideas easier to understand is for the writer to combine the two actions more concisely: "The defendant apologized to the plaintiff right after the jury found him liable for trespassing." (Note that both alternatives eliminated the passive voice.)

A third way to improve readability is the use of parallel grammar structure when making comparisons and when presenting items in a list. Parallel grammar structure means that the items being compared or the items in a list are all in the same form (i.e., all nouns, all verbs in the same tense, etc.). When making a comparison, the writer should strive for balance—the items being compared should be presented in parallel form, making it easier for the reader to see the comparison. For example: "The defendant separating the responsive and privileged documents is similar to *the defendant* in the Smith case" seems to compare an action (separating) to a person (the defendant). Consider instead, "The defendant separating the responsive and privileged documents is similar to the defendant in the Smith case separating the responsive and privileged documents." Although the latter sentence is longer, the comparison is more obvious because both sides of "is similar to" are worded identically.

Similarly, for items in a list or series, parallel grammar structure for all the items in the list ensures the reader can follow the writer's intended meaning. For example: "The lawyer was questioning the client, took a phone call, and had researched the issue" versus "The lawyer questioned the client, took a phone call, and researched the issue." Here, the parallelism is obvious in the second sentence by using the simple past tense for all the actions in the list. Using parallel grammatical structures makes the ideas easy for a reader to see and understand.

A fourth characteristic of readability is to avoid the use of nominalizations. A "nominalization" results when the writer replaces a strong verb with the noun form of the word, usually a noun ending in "ion," "ent," or "ant." For example, instead of saying, "The attorney argued," a nominalization would be, "The attorney made an argument." In addition to adding unnecessary words to a sentence, the use of nominalizations makes a reader do more work to understand the meaning than the use of the appropriate, stronger verb.

A fifth characteristic of effective readability is to avoid the use of "legalese," which often relies on outdated, pretentious terms. Some writers think that using legalese makes their sentences sound more sophisticated, but if we want to make a reader, especially one who may not be a lawyer, easily understand an idea, we want to avoid legalese. Even when writing for fellow lawyers, legalese merely clutters or distracts from the legal discussion or analysis, and it should not be confused with "legal terms of art."[19] Here are two examples of legalese: (1) "said" (as in the "said contract") versus simply "the contract" or "this contract" and (2) "the letter concerning the matter of" versus simply "the letter is about."[20] (Note that the rephrasing of each legalese expression is more straightforward and easier to understand.)

Finally, a sixth characteristic of readability is to avoid shifting verb tenses unless absolutely necessary. Readability requires the writer to avoid unnecessary shifts with verb tenses because verb tense shifts confuse a reader. Many languages do not have verb tenses and writers show time in other ways. English, though, is heavily dependent on verb tense as a way of conveying the time something happens. A reader uses verb tenses to situate the action or idea. Abruptly shifting the verb tenses in a unit of discourse confuses the reader. If a change in tense/time is needed, the writer needs to clearly mark this for a reader by referring to time or using a time expression like "before," "after," "as soon as," "meanwhile," etc.

For lawyers in practice, here are two simple "rules" about verb tense they should follow: (1) use simple present tense when stating legal rules and principles, as well as when stating thesis sentences for legal analyses and argument points and (2) use simple past tense when describing the facts, analyses, and holdings in a case.

d. Conciseness

A fourth characteristic, or goal, of "good" legal writing is conciseness. Conciseness—or brevity—is critical to effective legal writing.[21] Readers do not want to spend more time than necessary to understand a piece of writing. Professors, lawyers, judges, and justices are very busy people: they want to be able to see the ideas in your writing by reading as few words as possible. Brevity, though, is also the most difficult characteristic to balance with the other three—accuracy, clarity, and readability. When asked, many judges and justices,[22] especially on appellate courts, often reply that virtually all of the briefs they read would be more effective if the lawyers made their points more

---

19. *See* footnote 12, *supra,* this chapter. "One secret of good legal writing is to distinguish rigorously between terms of art and mere [legalese]." Garner, *supra* at 873.

20. Some additional examples include terms such as "heretofore," "hereinafter," and "the party of the first part." *See also* Bouchoux, *supra,* Ch. 4 § E.5, pp.121–25 (especially the table on pp. 124–25).

21. "Conciseness" means "being brief, but meaningful." Bouchoux, *supra,* p. 134.

22. In the United States, the term "justice" is used when referring to the judges on a supreme court in a jurisdiction, while the term "judge" is used for all other courts.

concisely, with fewer words.[23] Moreover, all courts have local rules applicable to the submission of briefs to the court. These rules include limits on the size of the briefs that can be submitted for motions and appeals; these limits are based on either the number of pages or the number of words. Because of these limits, it is incumbent on lawyers to make their arguments as concisely as possible, while still being accurate, complete, and clear.[24] Many times, brevity can be achieved through careful revision, editing, and proofreading of a document.

When writing a document, in addition to using active voice, avoiding nominalizations, and keeping subjects and their verbs close together, legal writers can look for other opportunities to eliminate unnecessary words in their writing. For example, phrases such as "due to the fact that," and "with reference to" can be simplified to "because" and "regarding," respectively.[25] Also, legal writers can eliminate unnecessary introductions to their points and topics, such as "It is important to note that" and "The first point to be covered is." In the first example here, all the words, including the word "that," should be eliminated and the writer should simply make the point. In the second example, a simple "First," serves the purpose to introduce the point. Having more words does not mean that a writer sounds sophisticated. When a writer can make their point accurately in fewer words, they have usually done a good job revising and editing their document.

One additional caution to achieve conciseness is to understand the difference between "redundancy" and "repetition." We have stressed the use of repetition to help a reader easily understand an idea. However, "redundancy" is unnecessary repetition. Remember that legal writing is not creative writing, so legal terms of art will be used repeatedly throughout a document, as will parallel grammar structure for comparisons and lists, so there is likely to be quite a bit of necessary and appropriate repetition within a legal document. However, unnecessarily repeating the same legal analysis or argument is not helpful. When working on a document, it is helpful to work with a professor or colleague to see the difference between needed repetition for understanding and unnecessary redundancy. This is a skill that takes time to develop. But getting feedback from a professor or colleague can help you develop this skill.

---

23. *E.g., Precision, Conciseness, Simplicity, and Clarity: The Dos and Don'ts of Appellate Briefs*, 58 FDI For the Defense 44 (March 2016).

24. To exceed the page or word limits in the court's local rules, a lawyer must make a motion or submit a petition to the court requesting permission; these motions or petitions are not always granted.

25. For additional examples of wordy phrases with their shorter substitutions, *see* Bouchoux, *supra*, p. 135.

Another type of unnecessary redundancy is using "matched pairs" such as "cease and desist," "final result," "each and every." In these matched pairs, both words mean the same thing, so there is no need to say the same thing twice.[26]

We have listed, explained, and elaborated on four goals for an excellent legal document—as well as for all legal communication: (1) the writing must be accurate, (2) it must be clear, (3) it must be easy to read and understand after reading the document only one time, and (4) it must also be concise. This last characteristic—conciseness—often creates great tension with the first three characteristics. These are not the only goals for good legal writing, but working on these goals is a good starting point for improving your legal writing for a U.S. reader. Achieving these four goals will make your writing easy for a reader to understand in a culture where the burden for clarity is on you, the writer.

An Exercise for Practice

Take a careful look at a document you have recently written. Read through it several times, each time looking for ways that you can make your writing move closer to these four goals:

1. Where in my document could I make my words <u>more accurately reflect</u> my meaning?
2. Where in my document could I make the ideas in my document <u>clearer</u> for a reader to understand by <u>the order</u> in which I present my ideas and <u>the labels</u> I use to highlight what I am saying to my reader?
3. Where in my document could I increase its **readability** by:
   a. using the active voice,
   b. keeping my subject/actor and verb/action close together,
   c. using parallel grammatical structures,
   d. avoiding nominalizations,
   e. avoiding legalese,
   f. avoiding shifting verb tenses?
4. Where in my document can I be more concise? What ideas can I present with fewer words? Is there any redundance I can delete?

You might also have a colleague read over your document to check for these goals. Often it is easier to analyze someone else's writing than your own.

26. Bouchoux, *supra*, pp. 137–38.

C. Time Management and the Writing Process[27]

Before merely "diving into the work" and starting to write, the writer should plan their writing efforts to allow sufficient time not only to draft the document but to revise, edit, and proofread the document, probably several times, during and after the actual drafting. These are key steps to produce effective legal discourse, because very few people can produce a clear, accurate, cohesive, and easily understood legal document in one step.

This **time-management consideration** is important for all legal writers, but especially for law students. Very often students in U.S. law schools believe they can write papers at the last minute because they had been successful with such short turnarounds in their classes prior to law school or prior to their U.S. studies for advanced legal degrees, such as the LL.M. However, the demands of effective legal discourse, as described in this chapter and the next, require much more precision and attention to details to be successful than the effort required for success in prior courses. Usually, these details and precision cannot be accomplished with a fast turnaround from start to finish.

The successful legal writer needs to think of writing as a process, and a process needs a beginning, a middle, and an end. At the beginning, the writer must first identify the idea or topic for the document—for example, the topic of a paper for a law school class, the client's potential legal issues for an office memorandum, or the reasons for a motion or an appeal to a court. Once the topic/idea has been identified, the writer should progress through the steps listed below, which comprise the middle of the writing process.

1. Organizing/Outlining

After identifying the thesis/topic, the writer should develop a structure for their topic. This could take the form of a "formal" outline,[28] or it could be a simple list of the sections needed to fully set out the support for the thesis. This outline may change as the writer progresses with the document, based on the discovery of new facts, new insights as the thesis is more fully developed, new research discoveries, or the writer's decisions in the revision process, described below.

The writer should also ensure that the source materials are organized and ready to use as of this starting point, so the writer is not delayed searching for information as they begin to draft the document.

27. Baffy & Schaetzel, *supra,* Pt. 1, Ch. 1 § D, p. 60–61.

28. A "formal outline" is a written plan for a document showing the sequence and organization in which the writer will make their points/arguments; it usually includes more than a simple list.

2. *Drafting*

Once the writer creates an outline and has source materials ready, they should begin to write—knowing that this writing will not be the final product. The writer should start by following the outline, recognizing that the outline could change as the writer's thoughts about the thesis evolve. However, the writer does need to be careful not to stray into irrelevant side topics, which could undermine the writer's thesis or distract from the document's purpose.

3. *Revising*

Revise, edit, and proofread—to many people these mean the same thing; however, they are not, although all three are types of "review."

"Revising" involves reading through the entire draft as though you are the intended reader, looking for logical inconsistencies and unclear factual descriptions. Changes needed during this stage could include adding or deleting material, rearranging the sequence of supporting points, or possibly even rethinking the ultimate conclusion. This step could be thought of as a "macro" (large-scale) review.

4. *Editing*[29]

The next review step is "editing." During this review step, the focus should be on paragraphs, sentences, and transitions (when required)—closely review these to determine how easy it will be for the reader to understand what the writer is saying and to follow the writer's logic. Thus, the writer should focus on the clarity of the main idea/thesis, the degree and accuracy of the support for that thesis, and the completeness, cohesion, and clarity of the support.

5. *Proofreading*

The final step is proofreading. Here, the reader should focus on the small things—grammar, punctuation, spelling, and format. The writer should consider creating a checklist for each of these categories and then should slowly and carefully review the entire document for each checklist separately; in other words, if the writer tries to proofread for all four categories in one review, it is virtually assured that some—or many—issues will be missed. For many legally trained readers in the United States, carelessness with these details equates to careless thinking. When a legal writer is perceived as careless

29. For more details concerning editing and proofreading, see Baffy & Schaetzel, *supra*, Pt. 1 Ch. 5, pp. 155–78.

about details, the legal reader questions whether they should believe or rely on the writer's conclusions.

6. The End of the Writing Process

Once the writer is satisfied the legal document is accurate, clear, concise, and easily readable, one final review is recommended. The writer should take one last look at the overall format—the presentation of the material. Are the margins, font, headings, and line spacing consistent? Can the reader easily find/see the thesis/purpose for the document, as well as the individual supporting points? If the answers to these questions are all "yes," then the writing process is complete.

Chapter 5
Legal Logic, Legal Rules, and Legal Analysis

Introduction

"Thinking like a lawyer"—that's the phrase all law students hear throughout their legal educational experience—but what exactly does that mean? Primarily it means lawyers must think logically. They must be able to support their conclusions consistent with the jurisprudence in their jurisdictions so they can wisely advise their clients and successfully argue to a court on behalf of their clients. How does a lawyer accomplish this?

A. Legal Logic

In the United States, lawyers use three types of reasoning (logic), depending on the circumstances in a case. These are deductive reasoning, inductive reasoning, and comparative[1] reasoning. At the simplest, deductive reasoning takes the reader from a broad principle to a specific conclusion, while inductive reasoning is the process by which a lawyer uses particular principles to develop a general rule or another particular conclusion.[2] Comparative

---

1. "Comparative" reasoning is often called "analogical" reasoning, but the authors prefer to use the broader term "comparative" because sometimes the comparison may result in a distinction (difference) from a precedent case rather than a similarity.

2. Ruggero J. Aldisert, *Logic for Lawyers: A Guide to Clear Legal Thinking*, pp. 48–49 (3rd ed. 1997).

reasoning is exactly as the name suggests; lawyers compare facts from the client's case to facts in precedent cases to determine whether a client's case is similar to—or different from—the precedent.

By applying one or more of these types of reasoning using the appropriate rules, standards, burdens, and presumptions (described in section B in this chapter), the lawyer can predict or argue the likely outcome of the client's case. Section C will then describe the expected structure for legal analysis in the U.S. common law.

1. Deductive Reasoning[3]

Although legal rules are often developed through the evolution of narrow precepts into broader principles (inductive reasoning), the underpinning of virtually all logic is deductive reasoning—what is often demonstrated in the classic syllogism:

> All men are mortal.
> Socrates is a man.
> Therefore, Socrates is mortal.

Here, the first sentence is the "major premise"; in this case think of it as a legal rule. The second sentence is the "minor premise," here, a factual situation requiring the application of the rule. Finally, from these two premises, the final sentence—the conclusion—can be inferred—assuming that both premises are true. In law, however, the truth of one or both of the premises often requires proof before the final conclusion can be asserted, which is when inductive and comparative reasoning could be applied.

2. Inductive Reasoning[4]

Inductive reasoning, using particular principles to develop a general rule, could be used to craft either or both the major and minor premise when a premise is not clear. Unlike the conclusion from a syllogism, which must be true when both underlying principles are true, the conclusion from inductive reasoning is usually "more probably true than not true." Even with this probability, the conclusion reached through induction often can become the major premise in a deductive argument.

---

3. *Id.* pp. 45–47; Nedzel, *Legal Reasoning, Research & Writing for International Graduate Students*, pp. 86–87 (5th ed. 2012).

4. Aldisert, *supra*, pp. 48–51.

3. Comparative Reasoning[5]

Comparative reasoning in the common law refers to both analogizing and distinguishing relevant facts from precedent cases to facts in a client's case. Thus, the focus in comparative reasoning is on facts, not rules. When legally relevant facts from a client's case are similar to legally relevant facts in a precedent case, then the lawyer can infer that the result for the client should be the same as the result from the precedent case. Here, the lawyer is analogizing. When the facts from a precedent case are different in a legally relevant way from the facts in a precedent case, then the lawyer would infer that the result for the client's case would be different from the result in the precedent case. Here, the lawyer is distinguishing. A lawyer would always look first for similarities (analogies) to facts in precedent cases because proof through analogy is stronger than proof merely by distinction.

B. Rules, Standards, Burdens, and Presumptions

To understand the legal reasoning processes in the United States, a student must learn numerous new terms—virtually all of which are legal terms of art, despite often being misused. The types of key terms in a lawyer's arsenal of knowledge include legal rules, legal standards, legal burdens, and legal presumptions, each of which is discussed more fully below.

1. Legal Rules and Tests

Legal rules are "the law." They may derive from constitutional provisions, statutes (codes), regulations, or—in common law—from cases. Regardless of the source, legal rules govern behavior. All legal rules have components, either "elements" or "factors," depending on whether the components are required (elements) or whether they must be weighed or balanced with or against each other (factors). These components are connected using various tests, as described below.

The names of these tests are usually not used explicitly in legal discourse, but it is important to understand precisely what is required in a legal rule to demonstrate whether the rule is or is not satisfied. Also note that many laws (legal rules) include a combination of these tests.

---

5. *Id.* pp. 51–52; David S. Romantz & Kathleen Elliott Vinson, *Legal Analysis: The Fundamental Skill* (2nd ed. 2009).

a. Conjunctive Rules

Conjunctive rules are rules that use the word "and" to join elements or factors, meaning that all the components are required.[6]

EXAMPLE: A contract requires an offer, [and] an acceptance, and consideration between the parties.

This wording indicates all three elements are required.

b. Disjunctive Rules

In contrast, disjunctive rules provide options and will use the word "or."[7]

EXAMPLE: A defendant is guilty of burglary when they enter or remain in a building and they have the intent to commit a felony or a theft inside.[8]

Here, the legal rule includes is both conjunctive and disjunctive tests. The defendant must act without authority and must have an intent.[9] The action can be either entering" the building or "remaining" in the building, while the intent can be either to commit a felony or to commit a theft.

c. Declarative Rules

Declarative rules state simply that a certain action is required.

EXAMPLE: A driver must come to a full stop at a red traffic light.

d. Prohibitive Rules

Prohibitive rules declare that a certain action is banned/prohibited.

EXAMPLE: Many state and local jurisdictions have laws that prohibit dropping litter (garbage or trash) on public streets.

---

6. Note that when the rule includes a list of elements or factors separated with commas and with an "and" in front of the last item in the list, then all of those components would be required.

7. Similar to conjunctive rules, when the rule includes a list of elements or factors separated with commas and with an "or" in front of the last item in the list, then only one of those components would be required, although more than one could be proved.

8. A theft could be either a felony or a misdemeanor, depending on the value of the goods stolen. A "misdemeanor" is a crime punishable by less than one year in jail and/or a fine, while a "felony" is a crime punishable by a year or more in jail and possibly a fine.

9. Note that this means there must be an "actus reus" and a "mens rea" for this criminal statute to be satisfied; these two requirements are typically required in all criminal laws, both in civil law and common law jurisdictions.

e. Balancing/Weighing Rules

When a rule involves "factors," these components are most often either balanced overall or weighed against each other.

EXAMPLE: A defense against a claim for copyright infringement is "fair use," where the secondary user asserts they had a legal right to use the copyrighted material. In U.S. federal law, this defense requires the balancing of four factors: (1) the purpose and character of the secondary use, (2) the nature of the copyrighted (original work), (3) the amount of the original work used by the secondary user, and (4) the effect on the market for the original work. These four factors are examined based on the facts in a particular case and then weighed together to determine whether the secondary user has harmed the copyright owner.

f. Combination Rules

In addition, several of these rule categories may be combined in the specific legal rule that governs a client's case. See the example of the burglary rule in the "Disjunctive Rules" section above, because it is also a combination rule. Many legal rules include combinations of these rule and test categories, which is why a lawyer must carefully read the governing legal rule to ensure that each component is addressed—or excluded—as required.

g. Subrules

A subrule is a principle or definition that will assist the court in deciding whether an element or factor has been satisfied.

EXAMPLE: One of the elements for the burglary rule requires "intent" to commit a felony or a theft. In many of the precedent cases, the court explains that a completed theft or felony is not required, only the intent. The court continues by explaining that a jury would infer intent by examining all the facts and circumstances surrounding the event, such as whether the building stored valuables, whether a defendant gained an unauthorized entry into the building, whether a defendant was discovered holding any of these valuables, and whether a defendant fled when they were discovered.[10]

Discussion questions: For each legal rule below, identify what type of rule/test applies. Some of these rules will include more than one type of test.

10. This list of circumstances could be thought of as "factors" because not all of them are required, but together some of them would support an inference of "intent."

1. Speed limits for cars traveling through a school zone shall be 25 miles per hour.
2. A government issued identification is required to go beyond this point.
3. Except as otherwise provided in this Code section, it shall be unlawful for any person to carry to or to possess or have under such person's control while within a school safety zone, at a school function, or on a bus or other transportation furnished by a school any weapon or explosive compound, other than fireworks.
4. In the federal Family and Medical Leave Act,
    a. The term "eligible employee" means an employee who has been employed—
        (i) for at least 12 months by the employer with respect to whom leave is requested under section 2612 of this title; and
        (ii) for at least 1,250 hours of service with such employer during the previous 12-month period.
5. It shall be an unlawful employment practice for an employer to fail or refuse to hire or to discharge any individual, or otherwise to discriminate against any individual with respect to his compensation, terms, conditions, or privileges of employment, because of such individual's race, color, religion, sex, or national origin.

2. Legal Standards

Legal standards define how a court will qualitatively or quantitatively evaluate a motion or an appeal.

a. Motion Standards

The standards for three of the most common motions in a civil case are described below:

i. Motion to Dismiss

Under the Federal Rules of Civil Procedure, Rule 12(b)(6), a "motion to dismiss" is a motion to dismiss all or some of the claims alleged in a complaint for "failure to state a claim upon which relief can be granted." This motion would be filed by a defendant prior to filing the answer to the complaint, which is prior to the start of discovery, so no "evidence" has been collected. At this point, only the allegations in the complaint provide any indication of what allegedly happened. Accordingly, the court must assume that all of the allegations in the complaint are true, and then it must determine whether the plaintiff would be legally entitled to the relief demanded in the complaint.

As a practical matter, motions to dismiss are seldom granted, with courts preferring to let matters move forward, at least through the discovery stage.

ii. Motion for Summary Judgment

Rule 56 is the Federal Rule of Civil Procedure applicable for "summary judgment." The rule provides, "The court shall grant summary judgment if the movant shows that there is no genuine dispute as to any material fact and the movant is entitled to judgment as a matter of law."

This motion would be filed after the conclusion of discovery, prior to any trial. Either a plaintiff or a defendant can file a motion for summary judgment, and the lawyers would support the motion with arguments based on the relevant evidence gathered during the discovery period.

Motions for summary judgment are not frequently granted—likely because evidence can be interpreted differently by jurors even when it is "undisputed." However, summary judgment motions may be granted more often than motions to dismiss—likely because at this point there is evidence and not merely the allegations in the complaint.

iii. Motion in Limine (or Motion to Suppress)

A motion in limine is made prior to the start of a trial and outside of the presence of a jury to request that certain evidence be excluded. Although these motions are made most often in criminal trials, they can be made in civil trials as well. The standard here first requires that the evidence must be relevant to issues in the case, meaning that the evidence tends to make a fact more or less probable than such fact would be without the evidence.[11] Then, however, such evidence may be excluded when "the probative value [of the evidence] is substantially outweighed by the danger of unfair prejudice, confusion of the issues, or misleading the jury, or by considerations of undue delay, waste of time, or needless presentation of cumulative evidence."[12]

b. Appellate Review Standards

When a lower court decision is appealed to a higher court, standards of appellate review define the level of deference the higher court should pay to the lower court's decision. The particular standard of review for a specific appeal depends on the procedural posture of the appeal and whether the decision

11. Fed. R. Evid. 401.
12. Fed. R. Evid. 403.

addressed a question of law or a question of fact.[13] The standards described below are listed in the order of least deference paid to a lower court decision to the most deference.

i. *De Novo* Review

De Novo means "to start anew," and a *de novo* review applies to questions of law. Courts are concerned that the law is explained and applied correctly, so an appellate court will give no deference to a lower court's analysis and description of law when it has been challenged; the appellate court would provide its own analysis of the law, even if that analysis substantially agrees with the lower court's interpretation.

ii. Clearly Erroneous Review

A clearly erroneous standard of review applies to questions of fact and is a minimal standard of deference. This deference is based on the fact that the trial court judge presided over the trial, heard testimony, and is in the best position to understand the evidence. As per the U.S. Supreme Court, "A finding is 'clearly erroneous" when although there is evidence to support it, the [appellate court] is left with the definite and firm conviction that a mistake has been committed."[14] This level of deference applies to fact finding by a judge, a special master, or a magistrate, but such minimal deference does not apply to findings of fact by a jury.

iii. Reasonableness/Substantial Evidence

The reasonableness/substantial evidence standard applies in two situations—a jury verdict and a formal agency decision. For a jury verdict, an appellate court gives great deference to jury verdicts unless there is no substantial evidence to support the decision. The only time a court would reverse a jury verdict is when "no rational trier of fact could have found the essential elements of the crime beyond a reasonable doubt."[15]

For formal agency decisions, such as statutory interpretation and policy-making, an appellate court applies this substantial evidence review.

---

13. https://www.law.georgetown.edu/wp-content/uploads/2019/09/Identifying-and-Understanding-Standards-of-Review.pdf (last visited July 28, 2024).

14. *United States v. United States Gypsum Co.*, 333 U.S. 364, 395 (1948).

15. *Jackson v. Virginia*, 443 U.S. 307, 319 (1979).

iv. Arbitrary and Capricious

The arbitrary and capricious standard applies to informal agency decisions when such decisions provide an agency's explanation of its decisions; the appellate court examines whether that decision can be deduced from the evidence or whether it seems illogical or random.

v. Abuse of Discretion

The abuse of discretion standard applies to those decisions by a trial judge that are discretionary—such as whether to include a specifically requested jury instruction or whether to allow or deny certain discovery requests. This standard provides great deference to the court's decision. However, if the basis for the appeal is that the judge did not apply the law correctly, the appellate court will reverse the lower court decision and usually remand the case[16] for a redetermination.

vi. Mixed Questions of Law and Fact

When an appeal is premised on a mixed question of law and fact, the first issue argued by the lawyers on appeal is usually which standard of review should apply—*de novo*, clearly erroneous, or sometimes even the abuse of discretion standard. When the appellate issue requires primarily legal analysis, the standard will be *de novo*, but when the issue involves primarily factual analysis, the standard applied will be more deferential.

3. Burdens of Proof

The two main categories of legal burdens are <u>the burden of production</u> and the <u>burden of proof</u>. The <u>burden of production</u> indicates which party has the burden to prove the legal rule or a specific element of the rule; the opposing party does not have a burden to show that it is correct or justified in its actions. A burden of production may shift from one party to the other in some circumstances. For example, in a copyright infringement case, the original copyright holder has the burden to produce evidence showing that the secondary user copied some or all of the copyrighted material without permission. The burden of production would then shift to the secondary user to show, for example, that their use of the copyrighted material was a fair use (i.e., legally justified).

---

16. "Remand" means to send the case back to the lower court, usually for a new trial or hearing, or for additional fact-finding or analysis.

In contrast, the burden of proof defines the weight of the evidence required to prove the rule or a specific part of a rule. There are three primary burdens of proof in U.S. common law.

a. Beyond a Reasonable Doubt

"Proof beyond a reasonable doubt" is defined as the amount of evidence sufficient to prove that no other **reasonable** explanation could be derived from the evidence presented.[17] This standard applies most frequently in criminal cases.

b. Clear and Convincing Evidence

"Clear and convincing evidence" is defined as evidence that is "highly and substantially more likely to be true than untrue."[18] This standard is most often used in civil (non-criminal) cases, such as cases involving fraud, breach of contract, and intellectual property.

c. Preponderance of the Evidence

"Preponderance of the evidence" is defined as the amount of evidence that convinces the jury that there is a greater than 50% chance that the claim is true.[19] This burden applies in civil (non-criminal) cases such as those for personal injuries.

4. Legal Presumptions

A presumption is a legal principle that allows a court to assume a fact is true without any evidence.[20] Probably the most well-known legal presumption exists in criminal law—a defendant is presumed innocent until proven guilty beyond a reasonable doubt. This is what is known as a "rebuttable" presumption, meaning that the assumption stands until a legally sufficient amount of evidence is provided, which proves the presumption to be wrong. Some other examples of rebuttable presumptions include (1) a person in possession of stolen goods is presumed to know the goods were stolen and (2) a person who has not been seen or heard from in seven years is presumed to be dead, although there are many other rebuttable presumptions in U.S. law.

---

17. https://www.law.cornell.edu/wex/beyond_a_reasonable_doubt (last visited July 28, 2024).

18. https://www.law.cornell.edu/wex/clear_and_convincing_evidence (quoting from *Colorado v. New Mexico,* 467 U.S. 310 [1984]) (last visited July 28, 2024).

19. https://www.law.cornell.edu/wex/preponderance_of_the_evidence (last visited July 28, 2024).

20. Bryan A. Garner, *Garner's Dictionary of Legal Usage,* p. 704 (3rd ed. 2011).

The opposite is an "irrebuttable" presumption, sometimes called a "conclusive presumption." These also exist in U.S. law, but not to the same extent as rebuttable presumptions. For example, a law that prohibits anyone under the age of 16 from obtaining a driver's license presumes that anyone younger than 16 years old is not capable of exercising the necessary care and skill to safely operate a vehicle; this presumption is irrebuttable, unless and until a legislative body changes the law.

C. Structure for Legal Analysis

All of the above rules, tests, standards, burdens, and presumptions, as well as the deductive, inductive, and comparative logic constructs, are employed at various points in the course of a legal analysis or argument. While this can seem overwhelming and confusing at first thought, legal analysis in U.S. common law is quite structured.

Remember that good legal writing is reader friendly—the goal for the writer is to make it as easy as possible for the reader to understand the analysis or argument with only one read-through. To facilitate this objective, legal analysis and argument in the United States follows an expected structure, sometimes described using food such as lasagna or a Big Mac. Both of these are layered foods, and a consumer expects to see these layers before biting into them. If either of these foods were put into a blender, or stacked in an unexpected order, the consumer likely would reject them. The same is true for legal analysis that does not follow the expected sequence; jumbling the parts would not meet the reader-friendly objective, which could result in the reader rejecting the analysis outright.

The structure for legal analysis is often described using the acronym CREAC[21]:

C—Start with the <u>conclusion</u>. Legal readers (lawyers and judges, usually) in the United States want to know where the analysis will take them, so start with the result—either the predicted outcome in a legal memorandum or the argued-for outcome in a court brief.

R—After stating the conclusion, present the legal <u>rule</u> that will be used to reach that result.

E—Next, <u>explain the law</u>, most frequently using precedent cases to illustrate or explain how the law operates to support various points

21. *See* Appendix C, Figures A.1 and A.2 for illustrations of this structure in predictive and persuasive writing, respectively.

underpinning the conclusion. In this rule explanation, only the law is discussed; the client's case is not mentioned.

A—Then, apply the law to the client's facts, using comparative reasoning—comparing the client's relevant facts to relevant facts from the precedent cases. Many times writers use the exact words of the law when they apply it to the client's relevant facts, so the reader can easily see how the law applies to this set of facts.

C—Finally, restate the conclusion.

Different acronyms may be used when discussing the structure for legal analysis, for example CRAC or IRAC. For CRAC, the structure is essentially the same, but the "E" is not explicitly listed, although the rule explanation is understood to be included within the "R." For IRAC, the "I" indicates the issue (the legal question) begins the legal analysis rather than a conclusion, and there is no "explanation" of the rule included.

The CREAC structure is used for both predictive (objective) and persuasive analysis. Even court opinions use it, although the structure is much more obvious in the more recent opinions. The acronyms IRAC and CRAC are often used in particular to describe the structure used when answering essay questions on law school and state bar exams. In those two cases, professors and bar examiners typically do not expect the writer to include explanations of the law using precedent cases.

In addition to this overall CREAC structure, each case illustration in the rule explanation and each corresponding application of that point to a client's case also have an expected structure. For a case illustration in the rule explanation, the paragraph includes a thesis sentence, facts relevant to the point being illustrated, and the court's holding in the precedent case. For the application of the illustrated point, the paragraph includes a thesis sentence, the client's facts relevant to the point, an explicit comparison of the client's relevant fact(s) to the corresponding relevant fact(s) from the precedent case, and a conclusion about that point for the client's case. Table 5.1 below illustrates the organizational structures for rule explanation and rule application. Note the similarity of the two; this consistency is expected by legal readers, and it helps the reader to follow the logic and easily see the similarities or differences.[22]

22. When making the analytical points, a legal writer would make only an analogy or a distinction, but not both, with the same precedent case. Although a client's case will never have all the same facts as a precedent case, the writer must decide whether the precedent case more strongly provides an analogy (a similarity) or a distinction (a difference). Similar facts mean the client's case should have the same result as the precedent case, while different facts would mean a different result, so trying to illustrate both a similarity and a difference would leave the reader confused as to which conclusion is correct.

Table 5.1 Structures for Explanation and Application

Rule Explanation (RE)	**Component**	**Rule Application (RA)**
The thesis sentence tells the reader what the paragraph will prove, not merely the subject to be discussed (topic sentence).	Thesis sentence	This thesis sentence should "mimic" the RE thesis sentence by using the key fact(s) being compared.
What one to two facts will you compare in the RA, plus sufficient context for the reader to understand what happened and how/why the court reached its result?	Relevant facts and sufficient context for reader	What one to two facts you will compare, plus sufficient context for the reader to understand? Do not force the reader to flip back to the facts section to remember what you are talking about.
N/A	Fact-to-fact comparison	A simple, direct comparison of the key facts. If there is more than one key fact, use a separate comparison sentence for each.
What the court held relative to the point you are making, not to the entire issue.	Conclusion	State the likely/probable result for the client's case.

As shown in Table 5.2, the CREAC structure is applied for each element or factor in a legal rule. Thus, the analysis for a legal rule that includes three elements would look like the structure illustrated in Table 5.2 below. This is what is often called a "nested CREAC."[23]

23. *See* Chapter 6, Figures 6.1 and 6.2 for illustrations of this structure in predictive and persuasive writing, respectively.

Table 5.2 Nested CREAC—How the Overall Legal Analysis Fits Together

Overall Structure	**Structure for each element**	**Description**
C		Conclusion for the ultimate legal issue
R		Overall legal rule (each element of the rule will be analyzed—the RE and RA—using a CREAC structure for each element)
	C	The conclusion for the first element (heading for A)
	R	The rule for the first element
E	**E**	All of the RE paragraphs for the first element
A	**A**	All of the RA paragraphs for the first element, in the same sequence as the RE paragraphs
	C	Conclusion for the first element
	C	The conclusion for the second element (heading for B)
	R	The rule for the second element
E	**E**	All of the RE paragraphs for the second element
A	**A**	All of the RA paragraphs for the second element, in the same sequence as the RE paragraphs
	C	Conclusion for the second element
	C	The conclusion for the third element (heading for C)
	R	The rule for the third element
E	**E**	All of the RE paragraphs for the third element
A	**A**	All of the RA paragraphs for the third element, in the same sequence as the RE paragraphs
	C	Conclusion for the third element
C		Restate the ultimate conclusion for the legal issue.

Chapter 6
A Lawyer's Work Product—Common Law and Civil Law Examples

Introduction

This chapter provides examples of a lawyer's work product, incorporating what has been described in earlier chapters in this book. Section A examines a client problem under U.S. common law, providing an overview of the lawyer's planning and research process and then looking at a sample office memorandum (predictive writing) and a sample court brief for a motion for summary judgment (persuasive writing). Section B then examines a similar client problem under the German civil law system, also providing an overview of the lawyer's planning and research process, as well as an excerpt from a court document. The excerpt here provides the English-language description of what would be included rather than the actual German-language version of the document.

Because this book focuses on the transition from civil law to common law, the common law example provides a more detailed client hypothetical and more details showing the analytical structure in both a predictive and persuasive context.

A. Common Law Problem, Process, and Results—A U.S. Common Law Example

1. Client Problem[1]

The client is Katerina Forrester, who lives in an apartment. Forrester had gone for a jog in her neighborhood park when the weather suddenly began to change, so she started to return home. As she walked through the parking lot of the apartments, the wind picked up and several shingles blew off the roof. These shingles hit Forrester in the head, causing several cuts on Forrester's scalp and neck and on the side of her face, along with a black eye and bruises on her face and neck. As soon as Forrester got home, she called for help. An ambulance arrived within a few minutes, and the emergency medical technicians stopped the bleeding and took Forrester to the hospital for treatment. Forrester now wants to sue the apartment landlord and owner for damages.

2. Process

The lawyer would first need to gather all the information from Forrester, which would include talking with her and, if possible, talking with several of her neighbors. It would also be helpful to get pictures of the apartment building, particularly the roof. The senior lawyer in the firm who interviewed Forrester would then assign an associate attorney to write a legal memorandum (office memorandum) to evaluate the likelihood of success for Forrester's case. If that associate was not familiar with the law about personal injuries, then they would look for a secondary source, such as a legal encyclopedia or a treatise, to determine what options Forrester might have.

The relevant law here is tort law.[2] Tort law for personal injuries such as the ones in this example is governed by state law, not federal law, and virtually all states have statutes addressing torts.

Once the associate determines the relevant law, and that this law is statutory, she would begin her research by first looking at an annotated version of the state's statutory law.[3] An "annotated code" is one that includes relevant precedent cases listed alongside/following the actual statutory language.

---

1. The Facts section in Figure 6.1 include more details about the client.

2. A "tort" is a civil wrong, so the question is one of liability, not of guilt (which applies to criminal matters).

3. While print versions of some jurisdictions' statutes may not be annotated with lists of relevant cases, many of the commercial search engines now in widespread use do include annotated codes for the jurisdiction. Having relevant cases listed along with the code section can save considerable time in the research process.

The associate would then draft the legal memorandum for use by the senior lawyer to evaluate how likely it would be for Forrester to win her tort claim for injuries against the apartment complex. An example of such a memorandum is provided in Figure 6.1. Following the memo is an example of a persuasive brief, on behalf of Forrester, in opposition to the apartment's motion for summary judgment on her claim.

3. Objective Analysis—The Office Memorandum (Memo)

The office memo serves two purposes:

- It is a record of the client's entire case, at the time of its writing,[4] so the complete facts and legal analysis must be included. This allows any lawyer in the firm access to a concise overview of the issues and predicted outcome.
- The facts and discussion (the predictive legal analysis) can become the basis for motion briefs if litigation or alternative dispute resolution is pursued.

The example in Figure 6.1 is a full (formal) memo that might be written in a law firm. Many firms today have adopted less formal, more concise versions of the "office memorandum," but the example here provides a more comprehensive version of the expected structure for this type of document.

4. Persuasive Analysis—Motion Brief

The motion for summary judgement would be filed after the period of discovery was completed. Evidence gathered during discovery would be used in both Forrester's arguments in opposition to the defendant apartment complex's motion and in the apartment complex's arguments in support of its motion. Figure 6.2 provides an example of Forrester's motion brief.

B. Civil Law Problem, Process, and Results—A German Civil Law Example

In Germany, as an example for an approach in a civil law country, the way to deal with a client's question depends on the relevant statute for the legal issue. In general, the approach differs depending on whether the certain statute is a

4. If, over time, the lawyers learn new facts or the law changes, then the memo would need to be revised—or a new memo written—to address the new facts and/or law.

broad or narrow one. If there is no statute that applies to the specific case, the lawsuit would fail. Below is an example in which a narrow statute provides the relevant law.

1. Client Problem

Suppose the client was walking around in her neighborhood and suddenly a part of the neighbor's roof, which had been blown off by the wind, hit her on the head. The client had to go to the hospital to receive the proper medical treatment. The neighbor had not properly maintained his house for years. Now the client wants to sue her neighbor for damages, so she sees a lawyer to ask for legal advice.

2. Process

The approach in this instance is typical for a narrow statute because such conduct is generally not well known until the lawyer has to deal with it for a specific case.[5]

First, the lawyer must find the relevant statute that might give the client a chance to file a successful suit against her neighbor. Thus, the first step the lawyer must take is to conduct some research, usually with the help of a research database.[6] With specific keywords from the case, the lawyer searches for some information about the relevant sources for the case. The database should provide some information about relevant treatises regarding the legal issue. In these treatises the lawyer should find the relevant statute.

Here, the relevant statute is section 836 paragraph 1 of the German Civil Code.[7] Because it is a narrow statute that applies only to a specific scenario, the lawyer should find relevant cases that already have dealt with this issue to support the client's case. These earlier, relevant cases might be included in the treatises found in the initial search, or the lawyer may need to search again, this time

---

5. While codes in civil law jurisdictions are generally broadly drafted, there are some exceptions for specific factual situations, which is when a narrowly drafted, statute would apply. *See supra* Ch. 1, fn. 9.

6. In Germany it would be, for example, www.beck-online.de or www.juris.de.

7. Section 836 paragraph 1 German Civil Code states: "If a person is killed, the body or health of a person is injured or an object is damaged as a result of the collapse of a building or other work connected to a plot of land or the detachment of parts of the building or work, the owner of the plot of land shall, if the collapse or detachment is the result of faulty construction or poor maintenance, be obliged to compensate the injured person for the resulting damage. The obligation to compensate shall not arise if the owner, for the purpose of averting the danger, observed the care required in traffic."

looking for the specific statute. The databases will include cases that have been decided with respect to the relevant statutory section.

To support the client's suit in the best way, the lawyer should cite earlier cases that are similar to the client's case. The stronger the similarity, the more useful are these earlier cases to support the client's claim. Following these steps ensures that all the elements of the statute are satisfied to file a successful claim against the neighbor. Again, before filing the suit with the court, the lawyer should discuss the case with the client to get approval.

3. Persuasive Analysis—Court Documents

Figure 6.3 is an example of a document that would be filed in court for this claim. It has been translated from its original German, and the names and addresses of the parties and the attorneys have been changed to protect their privacy.

Discussion Questions: Think about these questions and/or discuss them with a partner.

1. Look at the following components of the documents and answer the following questions:
   a. How is the law presented?
   b. How does the lawyer frame the points of her argument?
   c. How are the documents organized?
   d. What specific language does the lawyer use to show the certainty of the outcome of her case?
2. What similarities do you see between the U.S. examples and the German example?
3. What differences do you see between the U.S. examples and the German example?

Figure 6.1 Office (Legal) Memorandum: Predictive Writing

TO: Senior Attorney
FROM: Suzy Associate
DATE: July 1, 2024
RE: Client File No. 24-513 / Katerina Forrester / personal injury / Georgia

---

QUESTION PRESENTED[1]

Under Georgia law,[2] could Katerina Forrester be successful with a claim for personal injury against Midtown Apartments, Inc. when she was injured by shingles flying off the roof of its apartment building, and her injuries required medical treatment?

FACTS[3]

Our client is Katerina Forrester, a thirty-year-old woman who lives in the Midtown Apartments, Inc. ("Midtown Apartments") in Atlanta, Georgia. In May 2024, Forrester went jogging in a park only a few blocks from her apartment. As she returned home, a gust of wind blew some shingles off the roof of the apartment building, and these shingles hit Forrester in the face and head. Forrester suffered several cuts on her scalp, neck, and the side of her face, along with a black eye and bruises on her face and neck. These injuries required medical treatment. She now wants to sue Midtown Apartments for her injuries.[4]

Forrester graduated from college with a degree in computer science, and she has been employed as a computer programmer for Google for six years. Forrester has lived in Midtown Apartments for about two years. Forrester was an avid jogger, biker, and tennis player. When she moved in, Forrester signed a one-year lease with Midtown Apartments, which is both the owner of the property and the landlord managing the property. She renewed that lease for a second year when the first year ended. The lease included a term requiring Midtown Apartments to "keep and maintain all common areas of the buildings in a safe and habitable condition." The lease also included

---

1. A Question Presented generally has 3 parts – the first indicating which jurisdiction governs the issue, the second succinctly stating the legal question, and the third providing 2-3 key facts relevant to the issue. Note that these are facts, not legal conclusions.

2. Virtually all tort claims for personal injuries are covered by state law, not federal law, so the writer should include the applicable state jurisdiction.

3. The Facts section must be complete – include all the details known at the time the memo is written. However, the Facts should not include any argument or legal conclusions; these belong in the Discussion Section.

4. This first (introduction) paragraph provides a very brief context for the issue.

a term requiring Forrester to "keep and maintain" the interior areas of her apartment in a safe and habitable condition."[5]

During the first year in her apartment, Forrester complained numerous times about building "debris" in the parking lots and grounds of Midtown Apartments. This "debris" included roof shingles, nails, pieces of wood from window and door frames, and shattered glass from windows. While such debris was eventually cleaned up after each complaint, it has continued to appear at various times. Also, it often took 5-8 days after a complaint before the debris was cleaned up. Forrester has some pictures of this debris. In addition, Forrester knows of at least three other tenants who made such complaints, and they have offered to provide statements about the conditions at Midtown Apartments if Forrester goes forward with a lawsuit.

On May 28, 2024, Forrester decided to jog around the park that was only a few blocks from her apartment. After about twenty minutes of jogging, she noticed the wind began blowing and that clouds were moving closer, looking like it might rain, so she headed back to her apartment. As she walked through the parking lot for the apartment complex, a gust of wind arose and several of the asphalt shingles blew off the roof of one of the apartment buildings. These shingles hit Forrester in the face, scalp, and neck. She suffered a gash on her scalp and a pretty deep cut on the back of her neck. She also had cuts and bruises on her face and neck, as well as a black eye.

Forrester made it into her apartment, but because the cuts on her scalp and neck were bleeding rather heavily, she called for an ambulance. When the ambulance arrived, the emergency medical technicians ("EMT's") stopped the bleeding, but insisted she go to the hospital emergency room. Once there, the doctor on staff treated the cuts, which required eight stitches in her scalp and twelve stitches in her nek. She was also treated for the black eye and the other scrapes and bruises. All of this medical treatment has cost Forrester more than $15,000 in medical bills so far. In addition, Forrester has had to discontinue her biking, jogging, and tennis activities while she heals.

Forrester now wants to sue Midtown Apartments for her injuries, which would be a tort claim, based on "premises liability."[6]

---

5. When the client is a person, it is helpful to provide some background about the client immediately following the introduction.

6. "Premises liability" is a term used to indicate liability would apply to the owner / occupier of the land, which in this case that would be Midtown Apartments. Also, this last sentence in the Facts is a "transition" sentence. It indicates to the reader that the client's "story" is complete, and the legal analysis (the Discussion) will follow.

DISCUSSION

Katerina Forrester probably would be successful with a tort claim against Midtown Apartments, Inc. for damages resulting from her injuries.

A tort is the unlawful violation of a private legal right, other than from a breach of contract. O.C.G.A. § 51-1-1 (2024).[7] When the law requires a defendant to perform an act beneficial to another, or to refrain from doing an act that may injure another, then the injured party may recover from this breach if she suffers damages. O.C.G.A. § 51-1-6 (2024). Taken together, these two statutes provide a general legal rule necessary to analyze the negligence claim in this case; stated simply, this rule provides that a defendant is liable for a plaintiff's injuries when (a) the defendant owed a duty of care to the plaintiff, (b) the defendant breached that duty, (c) the plaintiff suffered injuries, and (d) the breach was the direct and proximate cause of the injuries.

In a case concerning premises liability, the Georgia code provides specifically, "Where an owner or occupier of land, by express or implied invitation,[8] induces or leads another to come upon [their] premises for any lawful purpose, [they] are liable to such persons for injuries caused by his failure to exercise ordinary case in the keeping the premises and approaches safe." O.C.G.A. § 51-3-1 (2024). Stated in lay terms, a landlord is liable to a tenant for injuries caused by the landlord's failure to exercise ordinary care to keep the common areas of the premises safe. *Id.*; *Commerce Properties, Inc.*[9] *v. Linthicum*, 434 S.E.2d 769 (Ga. Ct. App. 1993)(explaining that liability is based on O.C.G.A. § 51-3-1 when the injury occurred in the common areas of the property and not in the living areas controlled by the tenant).

In this case, there is no question that Midtown Apartments owed a duty of ordinary care to Forrester. First, Georgia law imposes such duty. O.C.G.A. § 51-3-1. Then, the lease signed by Forrester and Midtown Apartments included a term requiring Midtown Apartments to "keep and maintain all common areas of the buildings in a safe and habitable condition." O.C.G.A. § 51-1-8 (2024) ("duties may arise from [a] statute or from relations created by contract). Thus, there is no question that Midtown Apartments owed a duty of ordinary care to Forrester.

---

7. The abbreviation O.C.G.A. stands for the Official Code of Georgia Annotated.

8. A tenant leasing an apartment is considered an "invitee." *Behforouz v. Vakil*, 636 S.E.2d 674, 675 (Ga. Ct. App. 2006)(stating, "A landlord's tenant, for example, would be an invitee . . ..").

9. In this memo and the corresponding motion brief, the full names of the parities in case citations are spelled out rather than abbreviated according to Bluebook citation rules.

Further, there is no question that Forrester was injured. She suffered a gash on her scalp and a pretty deep cut on the back of her neck. She also had cuts and bruises on her face and neck, as well as a black eye. She required medical treatment for these injuries, incurring costs of over $15,000 so far. These injuries are documented with pictures, medical reports, and medical bills.

Thus, the two elements that are analyzed below are whether Midtown Apartments breached the duty of care to Forrester and whether that breach caused Forrester's injuries.

A. Midtown Apartments, the owner and landlord, probably breached its duty to maintain the apartment buildings in a safe and habitable condition.

A landlord is liable for a tenant's injury only when it has actual or constructive knowledge of the defective condition, it fails to repair that condition, and the tenant did not discover the condition through the exercise of reasonable care. O.C.G.A. § 51-3-1; *Mairs v. Whole Foods Market Group, Inc.*, 694 S.E.2d 129, 130 (Ga. Ct. App. 2010)(including the tenant's knowledge as an element of this analysis).

When a landlord knows or should have known about a dangerous condition, and the tenant could not know about the specific danger created by that condition, then the landlord is liable to the tenant. *Johnson Street Properties, LLC v. Clure*, 805 S.E.2d 60, 65-67 (Ga. 2017). In *Clure*, the tenant was struck by a tree limb that fell during a storm, lodged hanging from the gutter of one of the landlord's apartment buildings, and which subsequently struck her when the limb was removed from the gutter. *Id.* at 63. Tree limbs had fallen on the property before and had always been cleaned up by the landlord. *Id.* at 64. This time, however, the limb remained suspended from the gutter for some period of time, which was disputed by the parties. Further, another tenant, who had at times worked as a maintenance person for the landlord, decided to remove the hanging limb, and enlisted the tenant's help to warn other tenant's to avoid the area. Despite efforts to be careful, as the limb came down, it struck the plaintiff tenant. *Id.* at 65. The tenant sued the landlord for her injuries. *Id.*

The landlord moved for summary judgment, and the court denied the motion. *Id.* at 63. On appeal, the landlord argued that the lower court erred because the landlord had no knowledge of the hanging limb and that the tenant had superior knowledge of the danger. *Id.* at 64. Regarding the landlord's knowledge, the tenant alleged she left voicemails about the condition, and the landlord denied receiving such voicemails. The appellate court affirmed the trial court's denial of the landlord's motion for summary judgment because the disputed evidence about notice created a fact issue that should be decided by a jury. *Id.* at 65. Further, as to the tenant's knowledge of the danger, the court held that although the tenant knew about the general hazard of the hanging limb, it could not conclude as a "matter of law"[10] that "her knowledge of the specific hazard [of being struck by this limb] was equal to or greater than [the landlord's knowledge]." *Id.* at 67.

In Forrester's case, Midtown Apartments had actual notice about loose shingles on the roofs of its apartment buildings, and Forrester could not anticipate the specific danger of being struck by flying shingles. On several occasions prior to the events at issue here, Forrester and other tenants had notified Midtown Apartments about debris in the parking lots, including loose shingles from the roof, nails, pieces of wood, and broken glass. Moreover, while Forrester and the other tenants were aware that this debris could be a hazard on the ground, there is no indication that Forrester anticipated the specific danger of being struck by flying debris. Forrester's notifications to Midtown Apartments is similar to the tenant's notifications to the landlord in *Clure.* In addition, Forrester's lack of knowledge about the specific danger from loose shingles is similar to the tenant's lack of knowledge from being struck by the tree limb in *Clure.* Thus, Midtown Apartment probably breached its duty of care to Forrester.

A landlord's failure to make repairs within a reasonable time after notice is given renders the landlord liable to the tenant for damages resulting from the failure to make such repairs. *Ellis v. Hartford Run Apartments, LLC,* 779 S.E.2d 103, 107 (Ga. Ct. App. 2015)(holding there was a genuine issue of material fact precluding summary judgment for the landlord when the evidence was contradictory regarding tenants giving the landlord notice). In Forrester's case, she and several other tenants had notified Midtown Apartments several times about the "debris" found on the grounds of the apartment complex. However, because of the continuing instances of debris on the grounds, there is no indication that the cause of this debris, including loose shingles, was ever permanently repaired. Thus, Midtown Apartments probably breached its duty of ordinary care to Forrester.

B. Midtown Apartments' breach of its duty to Forrester probably caused Forrester's injuries.

A landlord is liable for a tenant's injury when the defective condition was the cause of the plaintiff's injuries. O.C.G.A. § 51-3-1.

---

10. The term "as a matter of law" here means that the evidence is undisputed and a reasonable person can reach only one conclusion as to its meaning. Thus, a jury must interpret the evidence to determine whether the tenant had equal or superior knowledge as to the risk of being struck by the tree limb.

A plaintiff in a premises liability case must present sufficient evidence of causation from which a factfinder could determine that the defective condition was the actual and proximate cause of the plaintiff's injury. *Riggs v. Highland Hills Apartments, LLC*, 779 S.E.2d 20 (Ga. Ct. App. 2015). In *Riggs*, the plaintiff tripped and fell on a piece of carpet covering a hole in a concrete walkway in the common area of an apartment complex. *Riggs*, 779 S.E.2d at 22. The plaintiff sued the landlord, who moved for summary judgment arguing, among other reasons, that hole was not the cause of the plaintiff's fall and injuries. Although no one witnessed the fall, the plaintiff presented the following evidence: (a) at the time of the fall, there was a two-inch-deep hole beneath the carpet, (b) the conditions around that carpet had existed for a considerable period of time, and (c) the conditions around the carpet were still there several days later. *Id.* at 23. Further, the plaintiff testified that "as soon as he stepped on the carpet the ground gave in and he fell." The court stated that such evidence specifically identified the defective condition and provided some evidence that the condition existed at the time and place of the plaintiff's fall. Thus, the court held that such evidence at least created a jury issue as to causation, and thus that summary judgment for the landlord was not appropriate. *Id.* at 24.

Here, Forrester has provided evidence about the defective condition and its causal connection to her injuries. Forrester has provided affidavits indicating (a) the ongoing problems with debris on the apartment grounds, which included loose shingles, (b) medical reports, with pictures, of her injuries, and (c) pictures of the shingles that struck her. Forrester's evidence is similar to the plaintiff's evidence in *Riggs*. Thus, Forrester has presented sufficient evidence to at least require a jury to determine causation.

Cause must be proved by more than just mere speculation. *Hobday v. Galardi*, 598 S.E.2d 350, 353 (Ga. Ct. App. 2004). In *Hobday*, the plaintiff suffered an eye injury at a shooting range. *Id.* at 351. At his deposition, the plaintiff testified about several possible causes for his injury, including bullet shrapnel and target shrapnel, although he never actually saw anything but a "quick shadow." He also had an expert testify, but that expert concluded only that he "could not begin to form an opinion of what struck" the plaintiff's eye. *Id.* at 352. The appellate court affirmed the trial court's grant of summary judgment for the defendant stating that the plaintiff offered no more than mere speculation and conjecture as to the cause of his injury.

In this case, Forrester has provided more than just speculation as to the cause of her injuries. Forrester has provided medical reports, with pictures, of her injuries. Further, she has pictures of the shingles that struck her. Forrester's evidence is more specific and thus different from the evidence in *Hobday*. Thus, Forrester has provided at least some evidence of causation.

CONCLUSION

Katerina Forrester probably would be successful with a claim against Midtown Apartments, Inc. for the injuries she sustained as a result of shingles flying off the roof of the apartment buildings. Midtown Apartments owed a duty of care to Forrester based on Georgia law and based on the terms of the lease she signed when she moved in, and which she renewed after one year. Midtown Apartments had actual knowledge of the problems with the roof because both Forrester and other tenants had complained to Midtown Apartments, and although the debris had been periodically cleaned up, it continued to occur.

Moreover, Midtown Apartments breached the duty to maintain the premises by its failure to maintain the roof in a safe and habitable condition, resulting in loose shingles being blown off and striking Forrester in the head and neck. In addition, there was no way for Forrester to know the continuing condition of the roof through exercising reasonable care. Finally, those loose, blowing shingles caused Forrester's injuries, which required medical treatment. Forrester's medical treatment cost her in excess of $15, 000, and meant that she was required to give up her athletic routines while she healed.

Figure 6.2 Motion Brief: Persuasive Writing

IN THE SUPERIOR COURT OF
DEKALB COUNT
STATE OF GEORGIA

Katerina Forrester	)	
	)	
Plaintiff	)	
	)	Case No. 24 – XXXX- JVN
	)	
v.	)	
	)	
Midtown Apartments, Inc.	)	
	)	
Defendant	)	

PLAINTIFF'S BRIEF IN OPPOSITION TO

DEFENDANT'S MOTION FOR SUMMARY JUDGMENT

Comes now, Katerina Forrester, by and through her counsel, and files this brief in opposition to Defendant's motion for summary judgment, pursuant to Rule 56 of the Georgia Rules of Civil Procedure.

In the following **FACTS** and **ARGUMENT AND CITATIONS TO AUTHORITIES** sections, Forrester proves that Midtown Apartments is not entitled to summary judgment because there are genuine issues of material facts and Forrester is entitled to have her claims heard and decided by a jury.

FACTS

This case is about a young, professional woman who suffered serious injuries caused by the negligence of her landlord, Midtown Apartments, Inc. ("Midtown Apartments"). Katerina Forrester ("Forrester") is a thirty-year-old woman who lives in the Midtown Apartments in Atlanta, Georgia. In May 2024, Forrester went jogging in a park only a few blocks from her apartment. As she returned home, a gust of wind blew some shingles off the roof of the apartment building, and these shingles hit Forrester in the face and head. Forrester suffered serious cuts on her scalp, neck, as well as bruises on the side of her face and a black eye and bruises on her face and neck. These extensive injuries required medical treatment, totaling over $15,000 thus far.[1]

---

1. Note how this introduction differs from the introduction to the Facts section in the Office Memorandum in Figure 6.1. The introduction here sets a more emotional tone, appealing to the court's sense of fairness and justice to show why Forrester is entitled to

Forrester is very physically fit. She is an avid jogger and biker, as well as a competitive tennis player in two local tennis clubs. However, while her injuries are healing, she cannot continue these athletic routines. She graduated from college with a degree in computer science, and she has been employed as a computer programmer for Google for six years.[2]

Forrester has lived in Midtown Apartment for about two years. When she moved in, Forrester signed a one-year lease with Midtown Apartments, which is both the owner of the property and the landlord managing the property. She renewed that lease when the first year ended. The lease included a term requiring Midtown Apartments to "keep and maintain all common areas of the buildings in a safe and habitable condition." The lease also included a term requiring Forrester to "keep and maintain" the interior areas of her apartment in a safe and habitable condition."[3]

During the first year in her apartment, Forrester complained numerous times about building "debris" in the parking lots and grounds of Midtown Apartments. This "debris" included roof shingles, nails, pieces of wood from window and door frames, and shattered glass from windows. This debris has continued to appear at various times, although it was eventually cleaned up after each complaint.[4] Also, it often took 5-8 days after a complaint before the debris was cleaned up. Forrester has some pictures of this debris, which she submitted with her affidavit during discovery. In addition, three other tenants made similar complaints, and they have provided affidavits about the conditions at Midtown Apartments and the recurring debris throughout the grounds.

---

win the motion (meaning Midtown Apartment's motion should be denied). This is known as a "theory of the case" or a "theme." It sets the tone for the remainder of the facts, "shading" those facts in a light favorable to Forrester, without the need for hyperbole or blatant emotionality throughout the details. Because persuasion should be subtle, a lawyer should avoid hyperbole, exaggeration, and "intensifying" (using terms like "certainly," "obviously," "indeed," etc. to emphasize [intensify] the point but without adding any substance to that emphasis) .

2. Notice here that the background about Forrester is a bit more detailed than what was provided in the memo, primarily to emphasize the negative impact her injuries have had on her life, but also because the firm learned more information about the client when investigating the case during the discovery phase.

3. This background about the lease terms is unchanged from the predictive memo; this information is simply factual, providing the terms of the lease, so there is no need to emphasize or enhance it in these facts.

4. Note this use of an independent clause for emphasis, with the dependent clause providing another fact. *See* App. D for more information about persuasive writing, generally.

On May 28, 2024, Forrester decided to jog around the park that was only a few blocks from her apartment. After about twenty minutes of jogging, she noticed the wind began blowing and that clouds were moving closer, looking like it might rain, so she headed back to her apartment. As she walked through the parking lot for the apartment complex, a gust of wind arose and several of the asphalt shingles blew off the roof of one of the apartment buildings.

These shingles hit Forrester in the face, scalp, and neck. She suffered a gash on her scalp and a fairly deep cut on the back of her neck. She also had cuts and bruises on her face and neck, as well as a black eye. Forrester grabbed some of the shingles that hit her before she ran back to her apartment, and she has submitted pictures of them with her affidavit for this motion.[5]

Forrester made it into her apartment, but because the cuts on her scalp and neck were bleeding rather heavily, she called for an ambulance. When the ambulance arrived, the emergency medical technicians ("EMT's") stopped the bleeding, but insisted she go to the hospital emergency room.

At the emergency room, a doctor treated the cuts. The gash on her scalp required eight stitches, and the deep cut on her neck required twelve stitches. She was also treated for the black eye and the other scrapes and bruises. All of this medical treatment – the ambulance ride, the emergency room treatment, the medications prescribed, and the follow-up care by her regular doctor – has cost Forrester more than $15,000 in medical bills so far. Forrester has submitted affidavits with the doctor's reports, including pictures, and the medical bills for all of this treatment as evidence in this matter.

Forrester sued Midtown Apartments. After the end of the discovery period, Midtown Apartments filed this motion for summary judgment. The following argument proves that this Court should deny the Defendant's motion and allow Forrester's case to be decided by a jury.[6]

---

5. This is the same information as in the memo but placed in its own paragraph for emphasis.

6. This transition differs from the transition at the end of the Facts section in the Memo; it states what the rest of the brief will prove, not merely what will be discussed.

ARGUMENT AND CITATIONS TO AUTHORITIES

Katerina Forrester has presented sufficient evidence to at least create genuine issues of material fact requiring this case to be decided by a jury because she could be successful with her claim against Midtown Apartments, Inc. for damages resulting from her injuries.[7]

A grant of summary judgment is appropriate when there are no genuine issues of material fact and the moving party is entitled to summary judgment as a matter of law. O.C.G.A.[8] § 9-11-56(c) (2024); *Lau's Corp. v. Haskins,* 405 S.E.2d 474 (Ga. 1991). When deciding a motion for summary judgment, the court should give the non-moving party the benefit of all reasonable doubt and it should construe the evidence and all inferences from that evidence most favorably for that non-moving party.[9] *Mairs v. Whole Foods Market Group, Inc.*, 694 S.E.2d129, 130 (Ga. Ct. App. 2010). Moreover, the non-moving party is only required to provide evidence that raises genuine issues of material fact; the non-moving party is not required to produce evidence demanding summary judgment in its favor. *Johnson Street Properties, LLC v. Clure*, 805 S.E.2d 60, 64 (Ga. 2017). In addition, most issues arising from premises liability are not susceptible to a decision on summary judgment. *Mairs*, 694 S.E.2d at 131.[10]

In Forrester's case, her claim is a tort claim arising from injuries incurred on the premises of her apartment. A tort is the unlawful violation of a private legal right, other than from a breach of contract. O.C.G.A. § 51-1-1 (2024). When the law requires a defendant to perform an act beneficial to another, or to refrain from doing an act that may injure another, then the injured party may recover from this breach if she suffers damages. O.C.G.A. § 51-1-6 (2024). Taken together, these two statutes provide a general legal rule necessary to analyze the negligence claim in this case; stated simply, this rule provides that a defendant is liable for a plaintiff's injuries when (a) the

7. In the brief, note first that the term "probably" is omitted, because the lawyer is arguing here for the stated result. Then, the reason supporting the desired result is included, which adds persuasion to the result.

8. The abbreviation O.C.G.A. stands for the Official Code of Georgia Annotated.

9. The "non-moving party" is the party opposing the motion.

10. This first paragraph explains the law required to decide a motion for summary judgment. The next two paragraphs then provide the law relevant to the specific claim at issue. The lawyers on both sides must provide and explain all law necessary to determine the desired result.

defendant owed a duty of care to the plaintiff, (b) the defendant breached that duty, (c) the plaintiff suffered injuries, and (d) the breach was the direct and proximate cause of the injuries.

In a case concerning premises liability, the Georgia code provides specifically, "Where an owner or occupier of land, by express or implied invitation,[11] induces or leads another to come upon [their] premises for any lawful purpose, [they] are liable to such persons for injuries caused by his failure to exercise ordinary case in the keeping the premises and approaches safe." O.C.G.A. § 51-3-1 (2024). Stated in lay terms, a landlord is liable to a tenant for injuries caused by the landlord's failure to exercise ordinary care to keep the common areas of the premises safe. *Id.*; *Commerce Properties, Inc. v. Linthicum*, 434 S.E.2d 769 (Ga. Ct. App. 1993)(explaining that liability is based on O.C.G.A. § 51-3-1 when the injury occurred in the common areas of the property and not in the living areas controlled by the tenant).

This brief will now prove that Midtown Apartments owed a duty of care to Forrester and that Forrester was injured. It will then demonstrate that there are genuine issues of material fact regarding whether Midtown Apartments breached its duty to Forrester and whether that breach was the cause of Forrester's injuries.

A. Midtown Apartments owed a duty of care to Forrester.[12]

In this case, there is no question that Midtown Apartments owed a duty of ordinary care to Forrester. First, Georgia law imposes such duty. O.C.G.A. § 51-3-1. Then, the lease signed by Forrester and Midtown Apartments included a term requiring Midtown Apartments to "keep and maintain all common areas of the buildings in a safe and habitable condition." O.C.G.A. § 51-1-8 (2024) ("duties may arise from [a] statute or from relations created by contract). Thus, there is no question that Midtown Apartments owed a duty of ordinary care to Forrester.

B. Forrester suffered injuries from the loose shingles hitting her.

Further, there is no question that Forrester was injured. She suffered a gash on her scalp and a pretty deep cut on the back of her neck. She also

11. A tenant leasing an apartment is considered an "invitee." *Behforouz v. Vakil*, 636 S.E.2d 674, 675 (Ga. Ct. App. 2006)(stating, "A landlord's tenant, for example, would be an invitee . . ..").

12. Note that this section A, as well as section B, are identical to two paragraphs in the introduction section of the office memorandum. The addition of headings, however, adds emphasis to these arguments, thus making the arguments more persuasive.

had cuts and bruises on her face and neck, as well as a black eye. The gash on her scalp required eight stitches, and the deep cut on her neck required twelve stitches. She was also treated for the black eye and the other scrapes and bruises. All of this medical treatment – the ambulance ride, the emergency room treatment, the medications prescribed, and the follow-up care by her regular doctor – has cost Forrester more than $15,000 in medical bills so far. Forrester has submitted affidavits with the doctor's reports and the medical bills for all of this treatment. This evidence proves Forrester was injured by the flying shingles.

C. Evidence shows that Midtown Apartments breached its duty of care to Forrester, which at least creates a genuine issue of material fact that a jury should decide.

A landlord is liable for a tenant's injury only when it has actual or constructive knowledge of the defective condition, it fails to repair that condition, and the tenant did not discover the condition through the exercise of reasonable care. O.C.G.A. § 51-3-1; *Mairs v. Whole Foods Market Group, Inc.*, 694 S.E.2d 129, 130 (Ga. Ct. App. 2010)(including the tenant's knowledge as an element of this analysis).

When a landlord knows or should have known about a dangerous condition, and the tenant could not know about the specific danger created by that condition, then the landlord is liable to the tenant. *Johnson Street Properties, LLC v. Clure*, 805 S.E.2d 60, 65-67 (Ga. 2017). In *Clure*, the tenant was struck by a tree limb that fell during a storm and lodged hanging from the gutter of one of the landlord's apartment buildings, and which subsequently struck her when the limb was removed from the gutter. *Id.* at 63. Tree limbs had fallen on the property before and had always been cleaned up by the landlord. *Id.* at 64. This time, however, the limb remained suspended from the gutter for some period of time, which was disputed by the parties. Further, another tenant, who had at times worked as a maintenance person for the landlord, decided to remove the hanging limb, and enlisted the tenant's help to warn other tenant's to avoid the area. Despite efforts to be careful, as the limb came down, it struck the plaintiff tenant. *Id.* at 65. The tenant sued the landlord for her injuries. *Id.*

The landlord moved for summary judgment, and the trial court denied the motion. *Id.* at 63. On appeal, the landlord argued that the trial court erred because the landlord had no knowledge of the hanging limb and that the tenant had superior knowledge of the danger. *Id.* at 64. Regarding the landlord's knowledge, the tenant alleged she left voicemails about the condition, and the landlord denied receiving such voicemails. The appellate court affirmed the trial court's denial of the landlord's motion for summary judgment because the disputed evidence about notice created a fact issue that should be decided by a jury. *Id.* at 65. Further, as to the tenant's knowledge of the danger, the court held that although the tenant knew about the general hazard of the hanging limb, the court could not conclude as a "matter of law"[13] that "her knowledge of the specific hazard [of being struck by this limb] was equal to or greater than [the landlord's knowledge]." *Id.* at 67.

In Forrester's case, Midtown Apartments had actual notice about loose shingles on the roofs of its apartment buildings, and Forrester could not anticipate the specific danger of being struck by flying shingles. On several occasions prior to the events at issue here, Forrester and other tenants had notified Midtown Apartments about debris in the parking lots, including loose shingles from the roof, nails, pieces of wood, and broken glass. Moreover, while Forrester and the other tenants were aware that this debris could be a hazard on the ground, there is no indication that Forrester anticipated the specific danger of being struck by flying debris. Forrester's notifications to Midtown Apartments is similar to the tenant's notifications to the landlord in *Clure.* In addition, Forrester's lack of knowledge about the specific danger from loose shingles are similar to the tenant's lack of knowledge from being struck by the tree limb in *Clure.* Thus, the facts in Forrester's case at least create genuine issues of material fact that Midtown Apartments breached its duty of care to Forrester, and this Court should deny the Defendant's motion for summary judgment.

A landlord's failure to make repairs within a reasonable time after notice is given renders the landlord liable to the tenant for damages resulting from the failure to make such repairs. *Ellis v. Hartford Run Apartments, LLC,* 779 S.E.2d 103, 107 (Ga. Ct. App. 2015)(holding there was a genuine issue of material fact precluding summary judgment for the landlord when the evidence was contradictory regarding tenants giving the landlord notice). In Forrester's case, she and several other tenants had notified Midtown Apartments several times about the "debris" found on the grounds of the apartment complex. Because of the continuing instances of debris on the grounds, there is no indication that the cause of this debris, including loose shingles, was ever permanently repaired, resulting in the loose shingles that struck Forrester. Thus, the facts in Forrester's case at least create genuine

---

13. The term "as a matter of law" here means that the evidence is undisputed and a reasonable person can reach only one conclusion as to its meaning. Thus, a jury must interpret the evidence to determine whether the tenant had equal or superior knowledge as to the risk of being struck by the tree limb.

issues of material fact that Midtown Apartments breached its duty of ordinary care to Forrester, and this Court should deny the Defendant's motion for summary judgment.

D. Evidence shows the breach by Midtown Apartments caused Forrester's injuries, which at least creates a genuine issue of material fact that a jury should decide.

A landlord is liable for a tenant's injury when the defective condition was the cause of the plaintiff's injuries. O.C.G.A. § 51-3-1.

A plaintiff in a premises liability case must present sufficient evidence of causation from which a factfinder could determine that the defective condition was the actual and proximate cause of the plaintiff's injury. *Riggs v. Highland Hills Apartments, LLC*, 779 S.E.2d 20 (Ga. Ct. App. 2015). In *Riggs*, the plaintiff tripped and fell on a piece of carpet covering a hole in a concrete walkway in the common area of an apartment complex. *Riggs*, 779 S.E.2d at 22. The plaintiff sued the landlord, who moved for summary judgment arguing, among other reasons, that hole was not the cause of the plaintiff's fall and injuries. Although no one witnessed the fall, the plaintiff presented the following evidence: (a) at the time of the fall, there was a two-inch-deep hole beneath the carpet, (b) the conditions around that carpet had existed for a considerable period of time, and (c) the conditions around the carpet were still there several days later. *Id.* at 23. Further, the plaintiff testified that "as soon as he stepped on the carpet the ground gave in and he fell." The court stated that such evidence specifically identified the defective condition and provided some evidence that the condition existed at the time and place of the plaintiff's fall. Thus, the court held that such evidence at least created a jury issue as to causation, and thus that summary judgment for the landlord was not appropriate. *Id.* at 24.

Here, Forrester has provided evidence about the defective condition and its causal connection to her injuries. Forrester has provided affidavits indicating (a) the ongoing problems with debris on the apartment grounds, which included loose shingles, (b) medical reports, with pictures, of her injuries, and (c) pictures of the shingles that struck her. Forrester's evidence is similar to the plaintiff's evidence in *Riggs*. Thus, Forrester has presented sufficient evidence to at least require a jury to determine causation, and thus this Court should deny Defendant's Motion for Summary Judgment.

Cause must be proved by more than just mere speculation. *Hobday v. Galardi*, 598 S.E.2d 350, 353 (Ga. Ct. App. 2004). In *Hobday*, the plaintiff suffered an eye injury at a shooting range. *Id.* at 351. At his deposition, the plaintiff testified about several possible causes for his injury, including bullet shrapnel and target shrapnel, although he never actually saw anything but a "quick shadow." He also had an expert testify, but that expert concluded only that he "could not begin to form an opinion of what struck" the plaintiff's eye. *Id.* at 352. The appellate court affirmed the trial court's grant of summary judgment for the defendant stating that the plaintiff offered no more than mere speculation and conjecture as to the cause of his injury.

In this case, Forrester has provided more than just speculation as to the cause of her injuries. Forrester has provided medical reports, with pictures, of her injuries. Further, she has pictures of the shingles that struck her. Forrester's evidence is more specific and thus different from the evidence in *Hobday*. Thus, Forrester has provided evidence of causation beyond mere speculation, and thus this Court should deny the Defendant's Motion for Summary Judgment.

CONCLUSION

For all the foregoing reasons, Plaintiff Katerina Forrester respectfully requests that this Court deny the Motion for Summary Judgment by Midtown Apartments, Inc.

Respectfully submitted this 10th day of October, 2024.

____

Attorney Signature

Figure 6.3 German Court Document (translated)

Attorney at law Wilhelm Müller Frankfurt am Main, 5 April 2023
Rathausstraße 5
60313 Frankfurt am Main
Hesse, Germany

Regional Court Frankfurt am Main
Gerichtsstraße 2
60313 Frankfurt am Main
Hesse, Germany

Statement Of Claim

by Werner Pohl, Kronberger Straße 11, 60323 Frankfurt am Main

- plaintiff -

representative: Attorney at law Wilhelm Müller,
Rathausstraße 5, 60313 Frankfurt am Main, Hesse, Germany

against

Optimal Bausatz GmbH & Co. KG, represented by Optimal GmbH, represented by its managing director Wolfgang Rist, Kronberger Straße 9, 60323 Frankfurt am Main,

- defendant -

representative: Attorney at law Holger Schmidt, Marktplatz 12, 60329 Frankfurt am

Main, Hesse, Germany

For: damages

Preliminary amount in dispute: EUR 6.000,-

In the name of and on behalf of the plaintiff, I hereby file a suit against the defendant. I request to set a date for an oral hearing, in which I will request to order the defendant to pay the plaintiff EUR 6,000.00 plus interest at five percentage points above the prime rate from the day following the date on which the action became pending.

Furthermore, in the event that the elements of Section 331 paragraph three sentence one of the German Code of Civil Procedure or Section 306 of the German Code of Civil Procedure are satisfied, I request that the defendant will be ordered as requested.

Reasons:

I.

The plaintiff was walking around in her neighborhood in Frankfurt am Main and suddenly a part of the defendant's roof, located at Kronberger Straße 9, 60323 Frankfurt am Main, which had been blown off by the wind, hit her in the head. The plaintiff had to go to the hospital to receive the proper medical treatment. The plaintiff had to pay EUR 6.000,- to the hospital for it. The defendant had not properly maintained its house, which it owns, for years. Now the plaintiff sues the defendant for damages.

II.

Pursuant to section 836 paragraph 1 German Civil Code the plaintiff has the right to recover the full amount of costs for her medical treatment (see Federal Supreme Court, 18 December 2020 – V ZR 193/19; Higher Regional Court Dusseldorf, 28 February 2018 – 19 U 17/17; Higher Regional Court Hamm, 5 February 2016 – 9 U 134/15; *Wagner*, in: Münchener Kommentar zum BGB, 5th ed. 2009, section 6 f.; for more details and further explanation see *Petershagen*, Die Gebäudehaftung, § 836 BGB im System der Verkehrssicherungspflichten, 2000). The plaintiff's health has been hurt when she was hit by a part of the defendant's roof. It had been blown off by the wind and hit the plaintiff in her head. The defendant is liable because it had not properly maintained its house for years. If it had maintained its house, and especially the roof properly, the tortious act would not have occurred and the plaintiff would not have been injured.

Evidence: expert opinion by Dipl.-Ing. Manfred Schneider dated 12 March 2023

Due to the plaintiff's injury, caused by the defendant, she had to receive medical treatment at the hospital. This caused costs of EUR 6.000,- which she had paid already.

Evidence: bill for the plaintiff's medical treatment, issued by Frankfurt am Main Hospital, dated 10 March 2023. Moreover, the defendant is the owner of the house from which the roof had been blown off.

Evidence: cadastral map excerpt regarding Kronberger Straße 9, 60323 Frankfurt am Main dated 12 March 2023

Therefore, according to section 836 paragraph 1 German Civil Code the plaintiff is entitled to recover the full amount of costs for the medical treatment (EUR 6.000,-) she already had paid.

Since the defendant - as it expressly stated – will not comply with the plaintiff's justified request, the plaintiff is required to file this suit.

There are no reasons preventing a decision by a single judge.
Should the court deem further explanation necessary, judicial notice is requested.

For the defendant, a certified as well as a simple copy of this statement of claim are attached for the purpose of service.

The advance on court costs according to a provisional amount in dispute of EUR 6.000,- was provided by electronic cost stamp.

Signature
Attorney at law

Appendix A
Answers to Questions and Exercises in the Chapters

Key Concepts 1, 2, and 3 are in Chapter 1. Key Concepts 4 and 5 are in Chapter 2.

Key Concepts 1

1. Classes at American law schools are characterized by the <u>**Socratic Method**</u>, and students sometimes get nervous about professors asking them questions over the cases they read.
2. Sometimes when examining the logic of a court's decisions in two cases, it's most helpful to look at the <u>**distinctions**</u> between two cases.
3. In many law schools, including some in the United States, professors conduct <u>**lecture**</u> classes, telling the students what they need to know about cases.
4. When trying to figure out how a client's claim will be decided in court, lawyers must look at <u>**precedent**</u> cases to see how judges have decided similar claims in the past. Lawyers then <u>**analogize**</u> their current case with precedent cases to see the similarities in the cases.
5. Making an <u>**analogy**</u> between two cases makes for sound, strong legal reasoning because similarities between your case and a precedent case show how your case will probably be decided.
6. The legal system in the United States is a <u>**common law**</u> system as principles in case law are applied as precedent to current cases.

7. After going over the cases in the assigned reading, the professor introduced several **hypotheticals/hypos** and asked students if these might be decided in the same way as the assigned cases.
8. Using **deductive** reasoning, we can examine a judge's past sentencings and get an idea of how long a defendant may be sentenced if found guilty.
9. Most countries have **civil code** legal systems, which rely more on applying statutes rather than precedent.
10. Sometimes lawyers use **inductive** reasoning when hearing a potential client's story; they put together the details of the story to figure out what happened in order to decide whether or not to take the case.

Key Concepts 2

1. One of the tasks for students in legal writing courses is to develop a **memorandum/memo** advising a partner in a law firm on the probable outcome of a case.
2. In the United States, a person charged with a crime could be prosecuted under both federal and state law for the same acts because of **dual sovereignty**.
3. In many countries of the world that have an **inquisitorial system**, the judge is involved as the case is presented in court, asking questions about the facts of the case.
4. Some people feel that a **bench** trial with a judge making the decisions is better than a **jury** trial because jurors can be too emotional.
5. The U.S. legal system is sometimes characterized as an **adversarial system** because the two parties argue the case without input from the judge.
6. The typical period of **discovery**, the pretrial time when parties exchange evidence they will present, is three to five months, though this can vary.

Key Concepts 3

1. An appeals court may **reverse** the decision of a lower court by substituting its own decision or by sending the case back to the lower court for a new trial.

2. In the American legal system, courts look at **precedent**, or past court decisions, for guidance when deciding cases.
3. In criminal cases, the proper **venue** is the locale where the crime was committed
4. The court included **dicta** in its opinion to illustrate factual situations in which the holding would not apply.
5. The U.S. Supreme Court **overruled** *Roe v. Wade,* a long-standing precedent in U.S. law, when it decided the *Dobbs v. Jackson Women's Health Organization*.
6. If a suit is filed in a place where the court does not have **jurisdiction** over the case, the suit may be dismissed.
7. In a case including several legal issues, a court's opinion will include the **holdings** for all the issues.

Key Concepts 4: Primary versus Secondary Authority

1. statutes **primary**
2. treatises **secondary**
3. American Law Reports **secondary**
4. cases **primary**
5. legal periodicals **secondary**
6. constitutions **primary**
7. legal encyclopedias **secondary**
8. regulations **primary**
9. restatements **secondary**

Key Concepts 5: Binding versus Persuasive Legal Authority

The Answer Key here indicates only whether the cases are binding or persuasive; the reader should review the text to determine the "why" (the reason it is binding or persuasive). Further, the reader should review the text to determine what factors influence the persuasive value.

1. The client's case concerns a question of federal law, and it is before the U.S. District Court for the Northern District of Georgia. You find the following cases, all of which address the same federal law at issue in your client's case, and you would like to use them to argue a motion on behalf of your client. For each case below, is it binding or persuasive? Why? If it is persuasive, how strong is its persuasive value?

A case from the U.S. Court of Appeals for the Eleventh Circuit? __**binding**__

A case from the U.S. Court of Appeals for the Third Circuit? __**persuasive**__

A case from the U.S. Supreme Court? __**binding**__

A case from the U.S. District Court for the Northern District of Georgia? __**persuasive**__

A case from the U.S. District Court for the Northern District of Florida? __**persuasive**__

2. Your client's case concerns a question of Georgia state law, and it is before the Superior Court of Fulton County Georgia (a "superior court" in Georgia is a trial level court). You find the following cases, all of which address the same state law at issue in your client's case, and you would like to use them to argue a motion on behalf of your client. For each case below, is it binding or persuasive? Why? If it is persuasive, how strong is its persuasive value?

A case from the Supreme Court of Georgia? __**binding**__

A case from the Georgia Court of Appeals? __**binding**__

A case from the Superior Court of DeKalb County Georgia? __**persuasive**__

A case from the U.S. District Court for the Northern District of Georgia? __**persuasive**__

A case from the U.S. Supreme Court? __**persuasive**__

Appendix B
Preparing for and Taking Law School Exams

Introduction

As described briefly in Chapter 1[1] and more thoroughly in Chapter 3, law school classes rely on reading cases and Socratic Dialog for students to learn the law. To actively participate in the discussions, students must prepare ahead of each class by reading and briefing the cases assigned for that class. During the semester, students should also take advantage of professors' office hours[2] when they have questions. Because course knowledge builds throughout the semester, students should not postpone asking for clarification for any materials they do not understand, thinking they can "understand this later." "Later" never seems to arrive, and suddenly it is time for the exam. Therefore, students might want to clarify any confusion or misunderstanding every week before moving on to the next week's reading. Confusion and misunderstandings can be clarified by attending class and listening to the discussion, visiting a professor during their office hours, or discussing cases in a study group. Having a clear understanding of course materials will also make it easier to "outline" the course materials, as described in section A, below.

Preparing for exams, however, requires a different focus by students than preparing for classes. In U.S. law schools, exam questions usually provide hypothetical fact situations requiring the students to answer one or more questions based on those facts—for example, predicting a likely outcome,

1. Chapter 1, *supra*, text at footnote 13.

2. Office hours are times set aside during the week when a professor is available to talk with students individually or in small groups. *Supra*, Chapter 3 § B.6.

such as what claims does A have against B and what defenses might B have. To be successful in this type of exam, students must know the legal rules—the rules for the area of law being tested—and then be able to apply those rules to the given facts.[3]

The following sections of this chapter describe "outlining" (a key step in preparing for law school exams), participating in study groups and practicing with exam questions, the types of exams and questions that may be included on the exams, and several time-management strategies for taking the exams.

A. Outlining, Study Groups, and Practice Exams

Outlining is the process of organizing case-oriented class notes into a cohesive summary of legal rules and principles applicable to the area of law covered in the class. From the case readings and class dialog, you will become familiar with how the courts have applied these rules to various fact situations, which you should have recorded in your class notes. By organizing those case-based notes according to issues or topics within the law covered in class, you sharpen your focus on what the legal rules are and how the courts applied these rules to facts to determine the answers to legal issues. Thus, it is the process of outlining itself where the learning occurs; although you may find a course outline from another student or an outline bank, merely reviewing someone else's outline is not as effective for your learning as creating your own outlines.

Although the term "outline" is used, there is no single correct format for you to follow when organizing your class notes. You might choose to use a formal outline structure, but you should also consider making a simple checklist, using a table or spreadsheet format, or even using a flowchart. You should determine what form works best for you as an aid to study for the exam.[4]

You should start outlining usually around three to four weeks after the semester begins; do not wait until the last few weeks of the semester. Waiting until those last few weeks to begin outlining leaves you with a daunting task because of the sheer volume of material, especially considering you are preparing for exams in multiple subjects. Further, turning case-based notes into rule-based (or topic-based or issue-based) outlines takes time and thought.

---

3. In most essay exam questions, there is no single "yes, there is a claim" or "no, there is no claim" answer. The students earn points toward the final grade by demonstrating their analytical ability, which means they must set out their reasoning, using the facts in the hypothetical to support their ultimate answer.

4. For more detailed information concerning creating law school course outlines, *see* M. Baffy & K. Schaetzel, *Academic Legal Discourse and Analysis,* Ch. 4, § B (2020).

Even if you use a commercial study aid as a guide,[5] it is the process of actually creating the outline that results in you mastering the material.

Another consideration when preparing for exams is participation in a "study group."[6] The study group could consider a "divide and conquer" strategy to develop a course outline, with each group member taking one, or a few, sections to outline, and then all the members sharing their section outlines. If this strategy is used, then prior to starting the outline, the group members should agree on a common format for the outline so the final product will be uniform. Format uniformity will allow the students to focus on content and avoid any distractions from form.

One additional activity that can reinforce your preparedness for exams is to practice answering sample exam questions. Such questions can be found in many of the commercial study aids, through "flash card"–style games available for many legal topics and often available in law school libraries, and in exam "banks" frequently maintained within a law school, either by the law library or through affiliation groups.[7] Some professors will even make some prior years' exam questions available for students, many with sample answers as well.

B. Types of Exams and Questions

Exams in U.S. law schools are virtually always written,[8] and for many courses, there is only one exam on which the final course grade is based.[9] In addition,

5. Commercial study aids take many forms and are available to purchase from many publishers, and thus are too numerous to list or describe in this text. Some study aids provide overviews and outlines of entire legal topics, such as torts, constitutional law, or evidence; some include examples of various legal documents as used in practice; and some even include sample exam questions, with sample answers. Virtually all law school libraries will have at least some commercial study aids available for students to review.

6. *See supra*, Chapter 3 § B.4 fn. 6 for a description of a study group.

7. An "affiliation group" is a student-led group of law students who share common interests or goals. These interests and goals may focus on an area of law, an area of law practice, or an ethnic heritage, to name just a few.

8. "Written" exams include both hand writing and using a computer. In addition, students studying for a Ph.D. or SJD degree in law are usually required to orally defend their dissertation.

9. There are some exceptions to this one exam = final grade structure. For example, some legal writing classes may grade smaller assignments during the semester and weigh them into the final grade; similarly, some clinical or transactional courses may involve group work on various projects throughout the semester.

some classes may require a final "paper,"[10] rather than a more "traditional test," as described below.

1. Take-Home versus In-Class Exams

There are two main categories of exams: take-home exams and in-class exams. Classes requiring a paper are a form of take-home exams, although a student may have several weeks to complete the paper. However, a take-home exam could be structured like a traditional test, but given for students to complete at home, often within a 24- or 48-hour period.

The more common type of exam is an in-class exam, given at a specific time and in a specific location (for example, a classroom). The duration of an in-class exam usually corresponds to the credit hours for the course—for example, a three credit–hour class would have a three-hour exam.[11] This type of exam could be either

- closed book, meaning the student may not bring any books or notes into the room where the exam is given, or
- open book, meaning the student may bring any books or notes into the room, or
- modified open book, meaning the student may bring in a specific book, such as a book of rules, like the Federal Rules of Evidence, or a specific document, like the student's course outline.

Each law professor determines which of these alternatives would apply for their exam. Each law professor also writes the exam for their course. For example, if there are three different professors teaching, each teaching a class on constitutional law, there will be three different exams.

2. Types of Questions

There are three main categories of questions that could be found on a law school exam—essay, multiple choice, and short answer.[12] Many exams will include all three types of questions, although some professors may choose to

---

10. The "paper" for a class could be a memo or a brief, as required in practice, or a scholarly paper on a specific legal topic for a seminar class. A seminar class is a small class, usually on a narrow topic or subset of an area of law, that is comprised of in-depth discussion on topics/subtopics within the ambit of the course subject.

11. In most law schools, students for whom English is a second language may be given additional time for an exam.

12. *See generally*, Baffy and Schaetzel, *supra*, Part II, Ch. 4 § C.

use only one or two of these types of questions. This section describes the categories of questions and includes considerations for organizing your answers. Section C then provides some time-saving strategies when taking exams.

Note that bar exams (state exams) will usually include a main section of multiple-choice questions (usually requiring one day, divided into two or three timed sections to take) with a separate day or days for essay questions (frequently four to six questions, 60 minutes each, with a break in between), and often a three- to four-hour section for a "performance exam."[13] Thus, the descriptions here and in section C are valuable for taking bar exams as well.

a. Essay Questions

There are three major types of essay questions, which are described below:

i. Issue Spotter

The most common type of essay exam in law school is the "issue spotter," which typically involves a lengthy (1–1 ½ pages) fact pattern (hypothetical) involving two or more persons or entities and a series of events and circumstances that involve one or more legal issues. The student could be required to "spot the legal issues" likely to arise between or among the parties and then predict likely outcomes for some or all of the parties, or the student could be required to draft a court opinion for a specified outcome related to one or more of the possible issues.

When organizing the answer for a single issue, follow the IRAC (or CRAC)[14] structure:

---

13. This type of exam tests a student's ability to organize a closed universe of documents (as they might encounter in practice) and to produce final written product as might be required in practice. For example, the given documents might include a memo from a supervising attorney in a law firm, selected transcripts of phone calls or depositions, letters from the client or between the client and the opposing party, selected cases and relevant statutes (the relevant law), as well as one page of instructions from that supervising attorney asking the "associate" (the test-taker) to produce a legal memorandum predicting the likely outcome of the client's case. This type of exam relies on an essay question, and this particular example would be an issue spotter, but note that the final product could be any type of essay. Eldon H. Reiley and Connie de la Vega, *The American Legal System for Foreign Lawyers*, Appx. B, pp. 453–54 (2012).

14. This IRAC/CRAC structure is very similar to the CREAC structure discussed in Chapter 5, *supra*. The difference is the "E"—the explanation of the law—which is done through the use of precedent cases and comparative reasoning. For an illustration of an answer using the IRAC structure, see Baffy and Schaetzel, *supra*, Part II, Ch. 4 § C.1.c, pp. 263–68.

I = issue (question) or C = conclusion (answer) for the issue.
R = rule—state the complete legal rule that is used to answer the issue
A = apply the rule, using the given facts, to support the conclusion
C = state or restate the conclusion for the issue

In the answer, some professors prefer that the issue is stated as a question; others may prefer the student to state the conclusion for the issue. By stating either one, the student is reminded of exactly what must be analyzed.

For the rule, state the entire rule, even if only some of the elements must be analyzed while others seem obvious. For any element of a rule that is "obvious," the student must provide the how or why—what facts or circumstances do not require any legal analysis to reach a conclusion. Providing this information tells the professor grading the exam that you did not merely forget to think about or address a part of the rule; thus, the student likely will get points for including this information.

For the application (or analysis), organize the answer by the elements of the rule—for example, by providing one paragraph for each element, and using the facts from the hypothetical to support the conclusion for that element. Was the rule satisfied or not satisfied? Here is where the student must be careful to avoid merely asserting conclusions—simply stating that an element was or was not satisfied will earn only the bare minimum number of points, if any. The answer must demonstrate what facts support the conclusion for the element to earn the full point value. In addition, any counterargument and rebuttal should be included with the analysis for the element when such counterargument could be raised. Similarly, any policy rationale that would support or undermine the predicted result should also be addressed. Including counterargument, rebuttal, and policy, along with facts applicable to the element, provides the basis to receive the maximum number of points for the question.

When the essay question requires the analysis of more than one legal issue, then the answer should address each issue using its own IRAC/CRAC structure. Here, you might also consider using headings—for example, a short phrase indicating which issue will be addressed following the heading. This is another means to make it easy for the professor to follow your answer, and thus for you to obtain maximum points for the answer.

An additional consideration with essay questions is to use the facts from the hypothetical in your analysis; do not write out a separate facts section before beginning your analysis. In addition, do not invent facts to fill in gaps in the story, and be careful about drawing factual inferences or conclusions, which can be considered as another means of inventing facts.

ii. Choice of Law

Another type of essay question that may be on an exam is a "choice of law" question, in which a legal issue and facts are presented, but for which there are two competing interpretations of the law. In other words, there is no precedent, or merely ambiguous or competing analyses in precedent cases. In this situation, the student is no longer merely an associate predicting the likely outcome of a client's case based on settled law but is now acting as an appellate court judge who must decide what the law is.

The structure for the answer to this type of question should (1) begin with an explanation that multiple competing rules (or interpretations) could apply, then (2) select the rule/interpretation that will be applied, with an explanation of why this version was chosen, and next (3) apply the selected rule to the facts, using IRAC/CRAC, and predict the outcome. Here again, the student might consider using headings as a means to make it easy for the professor to follow the student's answer.

iii. Policy

A third type of essay question could relate to policy—you would be asked to evaluate the purposes (policies) for a law and likely explain why you agree or disagree with the rule based on policy arguments. Here, you are likely acting as an appellate judge, or a law clerk to an appellate judge, who must evaluate the legal rule based on policy.

Here, the structure for an answer would begin with a direct response—a "yes" answer ("this is good law" or "this law should be adopted") or a "no" answer ("this is not good law" or "this law should not be adopted"). Then you should support this conclusion with two to four policy arguments.[15] Next, you should present competing policy rationales and rebut them, or at least minimize them. The answer should then conclude by reiterating the initial direct response.

b. Short Answer

Short answer questions are like miniature essay questions. Usually, a brief fact pattern is provided followed by a specific question. You would be asked to

15. Examples of policy arguments include social policy (e.g., safety or freedom), fairness and justice policy (i.e., treat everyone equally), economic policy (e.g., applying a cost-benefit analysis), separation of powers policy (e.g., deference to the legislature to create/amend law to address an issue), and judicial administration policy (e.g., decision would create or promote a rule making it less likely to overload the court system). Baffy and Schaetzel, *supra*, Part II, Ch. 2, p. 217.

provide a short answer, usually limited by word count or the number of typed lines. As with longer essay questions, you should first outline the answer (as described below), although here, the outline or checklist will be much shorter.

c. Multiple Choice

Multiple choice questions usually include a brief recitation of facts with a specific question posed about those facts. This facts/question format is followed by four or five conclusory statements, and you would be required to select the best answer.[16] While many students often think multiple choice questions are easier than essay questions, multiple choice questions can be tricky. These questions require you to read both the facts/question and the answer options very carefully. Further, if you select the wrong answer, you do not get any points, while with an essay or short answer question, you may get at least some points for an incomplete or inaccurate answer.

For multiple choice questions requiring the best answer, one strategy is to discard the obviously incorrect choice or choices and then focus on the choices that remain, which will often be just two options. Both of these choices may be "correct" but the student's job is to select the "best" choice.

C. Time Management Strategies for Exams

First—and very importantly—carefully read all the instructions. This includes where to place the student's name or number, whether the exam is timed and what that time limit is, and how to submit the exam when it is complete. Each law school has its own procedures and software, and each professor within a law school has their own exam-specific requirements, so the students must be careful to follow the instructions, or they risk getting no credit for an exam.

Then, look over the entire exam; this applies whether it is an in-class timed exam or a take-home exam. Students should get an overview of everything they are being asked to answer. Some professors may provide an estimated time to complete each question, which is only a guide, but other professors may not provide any such timing guide. The student should look at each question (essay, short-answer, and multiple-choice) and create a personal timetable to complete the exam based on their own ability and knowledge.

---

16. Reiley, *supra*, Appx. B, pp. 454–55; Baffy and Schaetzel, *supra*, Part II, Ch. 4, p. 282. Occasionally, the student is required to select "all" the statements that apply, but most often, the student must select the "best" answer.

This avoids a student spending considerable time on one question only to find later in the exam that they will not have sufficient time to complete other questions.

Next, for each essay question, you should read the "call of the question," which is the precise question being asked for that hypothetical/fact pattern.[17] By reading the exact question before reading the hypothetical, you save time because you can focus on the specific facts needed to answer that question. Moreover, reading the call of the question reinforces for you the precise question that is being asked, and thus helps you to focus your answer on that question.

Finally, before actually writing/typing an answer, you should briefly outline—or create a checklist—for your answer to each essay question. This will likely take only a minute or two but can save considerable time with the writing process. This outline/checklist also provides an opportunity for you to think through the entire answer to make certain it will be complete and will present the information in a logical and easy-to-follow structure. As you draft your answer, you can check off each point in the outline/checklist; this helps to avoid having to suddenly add or rearrange material, which risks omissions or odd logical sequences when trying to complete an answer under time pressure.

All of these strategies—both organizational and temporal—can help you achieve your optimal grade on an exam.

17. Although short answer questions involve a fact pattern/hypothetical, these are usually shorter than the essay questions and are less likely to include extraneous facts.

Appendix C
Note Regarding Persuasive Writing[1]

First and foremost, persuasion must be **subtle**—no one wants to accept any premise or argument point if they believe it is being forced on them. An argument will be much more successful when the writer convinces—or at least strongly suggests—that the desired result was the reader's idea and the writer is simply helping the reader realize this.

Persuasive legal writing in the United States is structurally similar, at a macro-level, to predictive writing for both legal analysis and the presentation of facts. For example, facts are virtually always more easily understood and followed when presented in chronological order. Similarly, the fundamental structure for legal analysis—CREAC[2]—applies for persuasive writing as well as predictive writing. That is, persuasive writing follows the conclusion, rule, explanation, analysis, conclusion organization, which is easy for a reader to follow and, thus, more convincing.

One sometimes surprising characteristic of good persuasive legal writing, however, is the minimal use—or even absence—of adjectives and adverbs, particularly adverbs referred to as "intensifiers."[3] Vivid details, precise word choice, and action verbs create persuasion—the writer must paint a vivid

---

1. This appendix provides a brief overview of persuasive legal writing—how it is similar to predictive legal writing and examples of some techniques used to create persuasion in facts and legal argument.

2. *See* Chapter 5.C, *supra.*

3. An "intensifier" is a descriptive word that adds emphasis to a noun, oftentimes without any supporting facts. Many judges and lawyers view such terms with suspicion, believing that the case at hand is weak because of the lack of details, factual or legal or both. Words like "clearly," "obviously," or "certainly" are the most frequent suspicious intensifiers.

picture for the reader using actual details, not vague description. Many people think that adjectives and adverbs are the most descriptive words in the English language; however, a writer can create a better picture with a precise verb or a vivid detail than with a list of adjectives.

Examples

Effective Persuasion	**Weak Persuasion**
The victim's home was on a half-acre lot. It was set back from the road, accessible down a winding driveway. The home was surrounded by large trees and dense shrubs, all of which blocked any view of the home from the road. The victim owned a 55-inch TV, two Apple iPads, and an Apple laptop computer. The TV was in the den, and the iPads and computer were on a large desk also located in the den. The defendant drove his dark blue Mazda Miata sports car down the driveway and parked close to the house, hidden by the shrubs. He pried open a window in the den, crept in, and disconnected the TV, iPads, and computers. He then hauled these items into his car and sped out of the driveway at a high rate of speed.	The victim's home was on a large, heavily wooded lot and not easily seen from the road. The defendant obviously broke into the house, found various electronic devices, loaded them into his car, and rapidly drove away.

In addition to vivid nouns and action verbs, below are some additional techniques used to successfully persuade in legal writing. In this context, it is important to remember that a lawyer must present **all** facts, both favorable and unfavorable. Omitting unfavorable facts negatively affects the writer's credibility; it creates a perception that the writer is lying, and it is a certainty that the opposing side will use such omissions against the writer's side of the case. In addition to using chronological order for facts, vivid details, precise words, and action verbs, the following techniques are helpful in persuading a reader:

- **Positions of emphasis**—placing favorable facts and arguments where they are likely to be remembered. This encompasses the concept of "primacy and recency" and the use of independent and dependent clauses.

- "**Primacy and recency**"—People generally better remember information that is presented first and last; information that is less favorable should be presented "in the middle," where it is less likely to make an impression on a reader. This is true both when presenting facts and when organizing the legal argument. For the argument, unless the logic in analyzing the legal rule requires otherwise,[4] the writer should consider addressing the strongest arguments first, followed by weaker arguments, and ending with another strong argument.
- **Independent and dependent clauses** allow the writer to juxtapose a favorable fact in the independent clause (a full sentence with a subject and verb) with a less favorable fact in the dependent clause (an incomplete thought/sentence). Example: The man stopped by the police was taller than the suspect based on the description, although the detained man did have blond hair, as did the suspect. *The emphasis here is on the difference—the height—and not on the similarity—the hair color.*

- **Details versus generalities**—More detail adds emphasis to what is written, while less detail de-emphasizes the facts or argument provided. (Review "Effective Persuasion" in the box above.)
- **Repetition**—Repeated use of key facts or action verbs adds emphasis. Example: The landowner **failed** to listen to the neighbors' warnings about trespassing children. He also **failed** to repair the gate allowing entry to his property, and he **failed** to put up any warning signs about the dangerous machinery stored on his property. All of these **failures** by the landlord indicate he **failed** to exercise reasonable care to protect trespassing children from the artificial conditions he maintained on his property. Thus, the landlord's **failures** prove he is liable to the families of the children injured. (The repeated word here, "fail," is used in both verb ["failed"] and noun ["failure"] forms. Use of different forms of the word allows the reader to maintain the emphasis of the repetition without repeating exactly the same word.)

The following legal memorandum and motion brief illustrate the similarities and differences between objective writing and persuasive writing.

4. For example, some legal rules have what is called a "threshold" element, meaning this element must always be addressed first. Other rules may require a particular sequence to analyze the elements in order for the analysis to make sense.

Figure A.1 Office Memorandum: Objective (Predictive) Writing

TO: Senior Attorney
FROM: Isaac Intern
DATE: April 4, 2023
RE: Client File No. 23–142; Jorge Klum; Constructive Eviction; Colorado

---

QUESTION PRESENTED

Under Colorado law, can Jorge Klum successfully assert a claim for constructive eviction against Metro Realty Corp. when he wrote letters describing the electrical, water, and rat problems, and he moved out before the end of his lease?

FACTS

Our client is Jorge Klum, a widower with four children, who leased an apartment from Metro Realty Corporation ("Metro Realty") starting in August 2023. After repeated notices and phone calls from Klum about problems with electrical power, water pressure, and rats, Klum began to withhold rent and then moved out. Metro Realty has now threatened to sue him. He has asked the firm whether he has any options against Metro Realty to allow him to move without continuing to pay rent.

Klum's wife died in 2020, and he is now raising his four children as a single father. He and his children have moved into a low rent apartment complex managed by Metro Realty. He signed a one-year lease with Metro Realty and moved in for the January 1, 2023, starting date.

Within a week of moving in, Klum realized there were several problems with the apartment. The electrical power periodically waned and surged, which ruined his microwave and destroyed his children's homework on the computer. The water pressure was inconsistent, and sometimes he had no water at all. When he did have water, it was usually cold. In addition, because the stove is electric, he generally could not heat water on the stove to bathe the children. This has been a problem trying to keep the children clean for school. Further, Klum has seen evidence of rats in his kitchen, as well as around the grounds of the apartment complex. With all of these problems, he is concerned about the health and safety of his family.

Klum has tried to get Metro Realty to fix the problems. He called Metro Realty several times in January, as well as several times in February and March. He also sent emails on January 28, February 7, March 1, and March 28.

Service people did come to his apartment on February 9. Although they knocked on the door, Klum's children were home alone, and he had instructed them not to let strangers into the apartment. On February 10, Klum called the management office to ask that he be contacted ahead of time for a service visit so he would be home to let the people in to make the repairs. However, no one answered, so he left a voice mail. Thus far, no one has returned his call.

Klum has now found a new apartment that he can afford, and he plans to move out on May 1.

Klum has asked what remedy he might have against Metro Realty.

DISCUSSION

Jorge Klum probably would be successful with a claim for constructive eviction against Metro Realty.

A landlord is liable for constructive eviction when the landlord's actions render the premises unfit for the leased purpose or deprive the tenant of the beneficial enjoyment of the premises, and the tenant abandons the premises within a reasonable time. *Radinsky v. Weaver*, 460 P.2d 218, 220–21 (Colo. 1969).

Metro Realty failed to repair the problems in Klum's apartment despite Klum's letters and phone calls. The courts have held landlords liable for constructive eviction when the landlords have ignored the tenants' complaints. *Id.* at 221. Here, Klum made several phone calls and sent four emails, but Metro Realty never corrected the electrical, water pressure, or rat problems. Thus, Klum gave Metro Realty repeated opportunities to correct the problems, and it failed to do so.[5]

This memo will now discuss whether Metro Realty rendered Klum's apartment unfit for its leased purpose and whether Klum abandoned the apartment within a reasonable time.

A. Metro Realty's failure to correct the problems after being notified rendered Klum's apartment unfit for its leased purpose.

A landlord is liable for constructive eviction when the landlord's actions render the premises unfit for the leased purpose. *Id.* A landlord's actions

5. Although not an explicit element in the rule, several cases in Colorado discussed "notice to the landlord" as though it were a requirement/element, so it seemed important to include.

could be acts of commission or acts of omission. *Eskanos & Supperstein v. Irwin*, 637 P.2d 403, 405 (Colo. App. 1981). Metro Realty's actions were acts
of omission.

Unresolved problems affecting the health and safety of the tenant render the premises unfit. *Kirkland v. Allen*, 678 P.2d 568, 570–71 (Colo. App. 1984). In *Kirkland*, the tenant signed a one-year lease for an apartment. Within about three months, the tenant refused to continue paying rent because of problems in the apartment. The tenant indicated the apartment had plumbing and structural problems, and it was infested with rodents. The infestation was so bad that the tenant and his wife often woke up with bites on their limbs. The court held that the landlord's failure to correct problems affecting the health and safety of the tenant rendered the premises unfit for the leased purpose. *Id.*

In Klum's case, the electrical, water, and rat problems threatened the health and safety of his family. The electricity periodically waned and surged, which destroyed his children's homework on the computer and ruined his microwave. The water pressure was inconsistent; sometimes he had no water at all. When there was water, it was usually cold. Also, because the stove was electric, he generally could not heat water on the stove to bathe the children. Further, Klum saw evidence of rats in his kitchen, as well as around the grounds of the apartment complex. The electrical, water, and rat problems in Klum's apartment are similar to the structural, water, and rat problems in *Kirkland* because all of these problems affected the health and safety of the tenant. Further, the failure of Metro Realty to correct the problems after repeated requests is similar to the failure of the landlord in *Kirkland* to correct the problems after repeated requests. Therefore, Metro Realty probably rendered his apartment unfit for its leased purpose.

B. Klum abandoned the apartment within a reasonable time.

A landlord is liable for constructive eviction when the tenant abandons the premises within a reasonable time. *Radinsky*, 460 P.2d 218 at 220–21. What constitutes a reasonable time depends on all the facts and circumstances in a case. *Eskanos & Supperstein*, 637 P.2d at 405.

When a tenant makes a good faith effort to work with the landlord to resolve the problems, the reasonable time period can be extended. *Id.* In *Eskanos & Supperstein*, the landlord and tenant entered into a two-year lease agreement for the tenant to operate a photography studio in the landlord's shopping center. *Id.* at 404. The tenant required a quiet studio to operate the studio successfully. *Id.* A restaurant was located adjacent to the tenant's premises, and two months after the start of the lease, the landlord leased the premises below the tenant to a dance studio. *Id.* The tenant repeatedly complained to the landlord that music from the restaurant and the dance studio, as well as from the shopping center stereo system, interfered with its business. *Id.* The landlord initially abated the noise problem, but the music from all three sources soon resumed. *Id.* The tenant vacated the premises eight months into the lease. *Id.* The landlord argued that no constructive eviction had occurred because the tenant failed to abandon the premises immediately after complaining about the noise. *Id.* at 406. The court affirmed the constructive eviction judgment against the landlord and explained that any delay in abandonment was the result of the tenant's good faith effort to work out a solution with the landlord. *Id.*

In this case, Klum promptly and repeatedly complained to Metro Realty in an attempt to get the problems resolved. Klum called the apartment manager several times in January, and again several times in both February and March, asking for these problems to be corrected. He also sent emails on January 28, February 7, March 1, and March 28 asking for the problems to be corrected. Service people came to the apartment one time, on February 9, but were not allowed inside because his children were home alone. Klum did, however, try to contact Metro Realty to arrange a time when he would be home for the service people to come, but Metro Realty did not respond. Klum's repeated attempts to have Metro Realty repair the problems in his apartment are similar to the tenant's repeated attempts in *Eskanos & Supperstein* to get the problems resolved. Accordingly, Klum made a good faith effort to work with Metro Realty to resolve the problems, and he probably abandoned the apartment within a reasonable time.

CONCLUSION

Klum probably would be successful with a claim for constructive eviction. First, Metro Realty's failure to correct the electrical, water, and rat problems rendered the apartment unfit for its leased purpose. Then, Metro Realty failed to correct the problems after repeated requests by Klum. Finally, Klum abandoned the apartment within a reasonable time because he first tried to resolve the problems with Metro Realty for four months but finally moved out when Metro Realty did not take any action.

Figure A.2 Motion Brief: Persuasive Writing

IN THE DISTRICT COURT OF
DENVER COUNTY
COLORADO

Metro Realty, Inc.,	)	
	)	
Plaintiff,	)	
	)	
	)	Case No. 23-XXX- NNN
v.	)	
	)	
Jorge Klum,	)	
	)	
Defendant,	)	

BRIEF IN SUPPORT OF DEFENDANT'S

MOTION FOR SUMMARY JUDGMENT

Comes now, Jorge Klum ("Klum") by and through his counsel and files this brief in support of his motion for summary judgment on his counterclaim for constructive eviction, pursuant to Rule 56 of the Colorado Rules of Civil Procedure.

In the following **FACTS** and **ARGUMENT AND CITATIONS TO AUTHORITIES** sections, Klum proves that Metro Realty should be held liable for constructive eviction because there are no genuine issues of material facts and Klum is entitled to judgment as a matter of law.

FACTS

This case is about a widower with four children trying to maintain a safe and healthy environment for his family to thrive. Jorge Klum is a widower with four children who signed a one-year lease for an apartment from Metro Realty, Inc. ("Metro Realty") beginning on January 1, 2023. Immediately after moving in, Klum discovered several serious problems with the apartment. He repeatedly tried to get Metro Realty to repair the problems, but to no avail. Despite his meager finances, Klum found a safer place to live and moved out on May 1, 2023. Metro Realty then sued him for rent due under the lease, and Klum counterclaimed for constructive eviction. After the completion of Discovery, Klum has now filed this Motion for Summary Judgment showing that Metro Realty's failure to repair the health and safety problems rendered his apartment unfit for its leased purpose and thus he does not owe any rent to Metro Realty.[1]

Within a week of moving in on January 1, 2023, Klum realized there were several problems with the apartment. The electrical power periodically waned and surged, which ruined his microwave and destroyed his children's homework on the computer.[2]

The water pressure was inconsistent, and sometimes he had no water at all. When he did have water, it was usually cold. In addition, because the stove is electric, he generally could not heat water on the stove to bathe the children. This has been a problem trying to keep the children clean for school.

Further, Klum has seen evidence of rats in his kitchen, as well as around the grounds of the apartment complex. With all of these problems, he is concerned about the health and safety of his family.

Klum has tried to get Metro Realty to fix the problems. He called Metro Realty several times in January. He also called several more times February and March.

Further, Klum sent emails on January 28, February 7, March 1, and March 28. Neither the phone calls nor the emails have resulted in many efforts to fix any of the health and safety problems that concerned Klum.

Service people were sent to his apartment on February 9.[3] Although they knocked on the door, Klum's children were home alone, and he had instructed them not to let strangers into the apartment.[4] On February 10, Klum called the management office again to ask that he be contacted ahead of time for a service visit so he would be home to let the people in to make the repairs. However, no one answered, so he left a voice mail. Thus far, no one returned this call.

Klum found a new apartment that he can afford, so he moved out on May 1, 2023. Metro Realty has now sued him to collect rent it alleges he owes

1. Note how this introduction differs from the introduction to the Facts section in the Office Memorandum, shown earlier in this appendix. The first sentence here sets a more emotional tone, appealing to the court's sense of fairness and justice to show why Klum is entitled to win the motion. This is known as a "theory of the case" or a "theme." It sets the tone for the remainder of the facts, "shading" those facts in a light favorable to Klum, without the need for hyperbole or blatant emotionality throughout the details.

2. This paragraph, and two following ones, say the same things said in the Facts section of the office memo; however, the use of short paragraphs – one for each problem – provides emphasis regarding the problems.

3. Note the use of passive voice here (were sent). This does not indicate any actor, which is a means to deemphasize this one call by service people.

4. Note the use of the dependent and independent clauses here.

on the remainder of the lease, and Klum filed his counterclaim for constructive eviction. Klum shows below that he is not liable for any rent because of Metro Realty's failure to make any repairs to problems threatening the health and safety of his family.[5]

ARGUMENT AND CITATIONS TO AUTHORITIES

Jorge Klum would be successful with a claim for constructive eviction against Metro Realty because both elements of the rule for constructive eviction are satisfied.[6]

A landlord is liable for constructive eviction when the landlord's actions render the premises unfit for the leased purpose or deprive the tenant of the beneficial enjoyment of the premises, and the tenant abandons the premises within a reasonable time.[7] *Radinsky v. Weaver*, 460 P.2d 218, 220-21 (Colo. 1969).

Metro Realty failed to repair the problems in Klum's apartment despite Klum's letters and phone calls. The courts have held landlords liable for constructive eviction when the landlords have ignored the tenants' complaints. *Id.* at 221. Here, Klum made several phone calls and sent four emails, but Metro Realty never corrected the electrical, water pressure, or rat problems. Thus, Klum gave Metro Realty repeated opportunities to correct the problems and it failed to do so.[8]

This brief will now prove that Metro Realty rendered Klum's apartment unfit for its leased purpose and that Klum abandoned the apartment within a reasonable time, thus satisfying both elements of the legal rule.[9]

---

5. The transition at the end of the Facts section in a court brief indicates what acts resulted in the case moving forward to trial and reiterates why Klum should win, reminding the reader of the language from the theme set out at the start of the Facts section.

6. In this brief, note first that the term "probably" is omitted, because here, the lawyer is arguing for a specific result. Then, the reason supporting the result is included, which adds persuasive support for the desired result.

7. This is the legal rule in Colorado that must be analyzed to determine whether Klum would be successful with a claim for constructive eviction. This rule statement is the same as the rule statement in the office memorandum.

8. This paragraph is the same as the corresponding paragraph in the office memorandum.

9. While the first two paragraphs in this introduction are identical to those in the office memorandum Discussion introduction, this last "roadmap" paragraph differs because it states what the brief will prove, not merely what is discussed.

A. Metro Realty's failure to correct the problems after being notified rendered Klum's apartment unfit for its leased purpose.[10]

A landlord is liable for constructive eviction when the landlord's actions render the premises unfit for the leased purpose. *Id.* A landlord's actions could be acts of commission or acts of omission. *Eskanos & Supperstein v. Irwin*, 637 P.2d 403, 405 (Colo. App. 1981). Metro Realty's actions were acts of omission.

Unresolved problems affecting the health and safety of the tenant render the premises unfit. *Kirkland v. Allen*, 678 P.2d 568, 570-71 (Colo. App. 1984). In *Kirkland*, the tenant signed a one-year lease for an apartment. Within about three months, the tenant refused to continue paying rent because of problems in the apartment. The tenant indicated the apartment had plumbing and structural problems, and it was infested with rodents. The infestation was so bad that the tenant and his wife often woke up with bites on their limbs. The court held that the landlord's failure to correct problems affecting the health and safety of the tenant rendered the premises unfit for the leased purpose. *Id.*

In Klum's case, the electrical, water, and rat problems threatened the health and safety of his family. The electricity periodically waned and surged, which destroyed his children's homework on the computer and ruined his microwave. The water pressure was inconsistent; sometimes he had no water at all. When there was water, it was usually cold. Also, because the stove was electric, he generally could not heat water on the stove to bathe the children. Further, Klum saw evidence of rats in his kitchen, as well as around the grounds of the apartment complex. The electrical, water, and rat problems in Klum's apartment are similar to the structural, water, and rat problems in *Kirkland* because all of these problems affected the health and safety of the tenant. Further, the failure of Metro Realty to correct the problems after repeated requests is similar to the failure of the landlord in *Kirkland* to correct the problems after repeated requests. Therefore, Metro Realty 's failure to repair the problems rendered Klum's apartment unfit for its leased purpose.

---

10. This entire Section A is the same as Section A in the office memorandum. The strength of the factual similarities does not require any "enhancements" to make the analysis / argument more persuasive.

B.Klum abandoned the apartment within a reasonable time.[11]

A landlord is liable for constructive eviction when the tenant abandons the premises within a reasonable time. *Radinsky*, 460 P.2d 218 at 220-21. What constitutes a reasonable time depends on all the facts and circumstances in a case. *Eskanos & Supperstein*, 637 P.2d at 405.

When a tenant makes a good faith effort to work with the landlord to resolve the problems, the reasonable time period can be extended. *Id.* In *Eskanos & Supperstein*, the landlord and tenant entered into a two-year lease agreement for the tenant to operate a photography studio in the landlord's shopping center. *Id.* at 404. The tenant required a quiet studio to operate the studio successfully. *Id.* A restaurant was located adjacent to the tenant's premises, and two months after the start of the lease, the landlord leased the premises below the tenant to a dance studio. *Id.* The tenant repeatedly complained to the landlord that music from the restaurant and the dance studio, as well as from the shopping center stereo system, interfered with its business. *Id.* The landlord initially abated the noise problem, but the music from all three sources soon resumed. *Id.* The tenant vacated the premises eight months into the lease. *Id.* The landlord argued that no constructive eviction had occurred because the tenant failed to abandon the premises immediately after complaining about the noise. *Id.* at 406. The court affirmed the constructive eviction judgment against the landlord and explained that any delay in abandonment was the result of the tenant's good faith effort to work out a solution with the landlord. *Id.*

In this case, Klum promptly and repeatedly complained to Metro Realty in an attempt to get the problems resolved. Klum called the apartment manager several times in January, and again several times in both February and March, asking for these problems to be corrected. He also sent emails on January 28, February 7, March 1, and March 28 asking for the problems to be corrected. Service people came to the apartment one time, on February 9, but were not allowed inside because his children were home alone. Klum did, however, try to contact Metro Realty to arrange a time when he would be home for the service people to come, but Metro Realty did not respond. Klum's repeated attempts to have Metro Realty repair the problems in his apartment are similar to the tenant's repeated attempts in

11. This entire Section B is the same as Section B in the office memorandum. The strength of the factual similarities does not require any "enhancements" to make the analysis / argument more persuasive.

Eskanos & Supperstein to get the problems resolved. Accordingly, Klum made a good faith effort to work with Metro Realty to resolve the problems, and he therefore abandoned the apartment within a reasonable time.

CONCLUSION

For all the foregoing reasons, Klum respectfully requests this Court to grant this Motion for Summary Judgement and hold Metro Realty liable for constructive eviction, awarding Klum all damages and costs to which he is entitled.[12]

Respectfully submitted this ____ day of ______, 2023.

Attorney signature

Discussion questions: Think about these questions and/or discuss them with a partner.

1. Which is the objective piece of writing, and which is the persuasive piece of writing?
2. What is the purpose of the memorandum?
3. What is the purpose of the brief?
4. What similarities and differences do you see in the organization of the memorandum and the brief?
5. What are the strong and weak arguments in the memorandum? Where are they mentioned?
6. What are the strong and weak arguments in the brief? Where are they mentioned?
7. What similarities and differences do you see in the language used in the memorandum and the brief? Can you give five examples?
8. What differences do you see in the conclusions of the memorandum and brief? How are these differences related to the purpose of each document?

12. The Conclusion section in virtually all persuasive court briefs (both motion briefs and briefs on appeal) is "fixed." It provides a simple, direct statement reiterating the result desired by the writer.

Bibliography

Logic for Lawyers: A Guide to Clear Legal Thinking
Ruggero J. Aldisert (3rd ed. 1997 National Institute of Trial Advocacy [NITA])

Academic Legal Discourse and Analysis
Marta Baffy & Kirsten Schaetzel (2020 WaltersKluwer)

Aspen Handbook for Legal Writers
Deborah E. Bouchoux (5th edition 2021 WoltersKluwer)

A Practical Guide to Appellate Advocacy
Mary Beth Beazley (6th edition 2022 Aspen Publishing)

Briefs and Beyond: Persuasive Legal Writing
Mary Beth Beazley & Monte Smith (2021 Aspen Publishing)

U.S. Legal Practice Skills for International Law Students
Anne M. Burr & Howard Bromberg (2014 Carolina Academic Press)

Legal Writing and Analysis
Linda H. Edwards (6th ed. 2023 Aspen Publishing Co.)

Just Writing: Grammar, Punctuation, and Style for the Legal Writer
Anne Enquist, Laurel Currie Oates, & Jeremy Francis (6th ed. 2022 WoltersKluwer)

Lost in Translation: Effective Legal Writing for the International Community
Kevin J. Fandl (2014 LexisNexis)

An Introduction to the Legal System of the United States
E. Allen Farnsworth (4th ed. 2010 Oxford University Press)

American Legal Systems: A Resource and Reference Guide
Toni M. Fine (1997 Anderson Publishing Co.)

Civil Procedure
Richard D. Freer (5th ed. 2022 WaltersKluwer)

Garner's Dictionary of Modern Legal Usage
Bryan A. Garner (3rd ed. 2011 Oxford University Press)

Legal Methods
Jane C. Ginsburg (5th ed. 2020 Foundation Press)
Elements of Law
Eva H. Hanks (2nd ed. 2010 LexisNexis)
The Law of the United States
Peter Hay (4th ed. 2016)
The U.S. Legal System: The Basics
Toni Jaeger-Fine (2021 Carolina Academic Press)
The United States Legal System
Margaret Z. Johns & Rex R. Perschbacher (2nd ed. 2007 Carolina Academic Press)
Writing around the World: A Guide to Writing Across Cultures
Matthew McCool (2009 Continuum International Publishing Group).
The International Lawyer's Guide to Legal Analysis & Communication in the U.S.
Deborah B. McGregor & Cynthia Adams (2008 WoltersKluwer)
Legal Reasoning, Research, & Writing for International Graduate Students
Nadia E. Nedzel (5th ed. 2012 WoltersKluwer)
Legal Analysis: The Fundamental Skill
David S. Romantz & Kathleen Elliott Vinson (2nd ed. 2009 Carolina Academic Press)
The American Legal System for Foreign Lawyers
Eldon H. Reiley & Connie de la Vega (2012 WoltersKluwer)
An Advocate Persuades
Joan Rocklin, Robert Rocklin, Christine Coughlin, & Sandy Patrick (2nd ed. 2022 Carolina Academic Press)
Overview of U.S. Law
J. R. Swanegan & Ellen S. Pogor (2nd ed. 2019 Carolina Academic Press)
Rhetoric for Legal Writers: The Theory and Practice of Analysis and Persuasion
Kristen Konrad Tiscione (2nd ed. 2016 West Academic Publishing)
Academic Legal Writing
Eugene Volokh (5th ed. 2016 Foundation Press)
Style: Lessons in Clarity and Grace
Joseph M. Williams and Joseph Bizup (11th ed. Pearson 2014)
Plain English for Lawyers
Richard C. Wydick & Amy E. Sloan (6th ed. 2019 Carolina Academic Press)

Index